500 YEARS OF LIES

The fascinating accounts of North America's and South America's Peoples are enough to captivate me on their own. When these events are set alongside what I was taught, the enchantment reaches a new dimension. I hope your wonder runs free inside these pages.

Dave

500 YEARS OF LIES

DISCOVER THE EXTRAORDINARY NUMBER OF NATIVE INDIAN GIFTS TO THE WORLD

DAVE PATTERSON,
the1492guy

PATTERSON AND CO.
TORONTO, CANADA

500 Years of Lies
Discover the Extraordinary Number of Native Indian Gifts to the World
By Dave Patterson, the1492guy
Published by Patterson and Co., Toronto, Ontario

For permission requests, write to the publisher, addressed "Attention: the1492guy" 42 Cartier Cr., Toronto, Ontario L4C 2N2

Original front cover design: Pixelstudio
Interior design: Wendy Dunning, wendydunning.com
Editors: Peter Wietmarschen and Colleen Wietmarschen, https://YourLiteraryProse.com
Book consultants: Peter Wietmarschen and Colleen Wietmarschen

ISBN: 978-1-7752550-0-0 (Paperback)
ISBN: 978-1-7752550-1-7 (eBook)

Published in Toronto, Ontario by Patterson and Co.

Printed in the United States of America
10 9 8 7 6 5 4 3 2 1

First Edition

*if this hybrid of self-development
exercise plus history resonates
with you, spread the message to four others*

Dedication

TEHANETORENS
Ray Fadden

KAHIONHES
John Fadden

KANIETAKERON
David Fadden

Clara & Dale & Ky have heard my rants

TABLE OF CONTENTS

SECTION 3
WHOSE CONTINENTS? *97*

≋ About the Cover ≋

Taino Indian sculpture, Isabela, Puerto Rico
It all started here, with the Taino of the West Indies. They were first visited in Hispaniola, today's island of Haiti/Dominican Republic. Will you insist that Columbus "discovered" the island, instead of "first visiting" the Tainos? It's just a word, isn't it? He did "discover" it, from the European point of view, didn't he? The question: do you want your kids or grandkids to be raised as world citizens with integrity, or do you want them raised to defend their ancestral turf, regardless of integrity issues?

Words are all we've got in a civilized world. They matter. In 1492, The Tainos of the West Indies were a thriving and advanced culture with 8,000,000 citizens, a group on the verge of attaining nation-statehood. Within 10 years, 60,000 of them remained. If that story interests you, remember that similar-themed stories are to be found by the hundreds, as the hemisphere was gradually "discovered."

≋ Preface ≋

Let's go back to 1999; I was sitting in my car listening to the radio. The voice I heard had such an impact on me. I was hanging onto every word. After listening to this voice, I was never the same again. How could this voice make such an impression after only two hours?

I was astonished by the information I was hearing about the gifts given to the world by people of the Western Hemisphere. But just as important, I was surprised by my own ignorance. I had trusted our Western educational system. The most shocking part was I had thought I was prepared to proceed through life with a fair and accurate view of my world. So why didn't I know everything I needed to know to have a clear view of the world? I believed I was wired and ready to go.

The man behind the voice on my radio was Ray Fadden. He had been recorded in 1975 at his Six Nations Indian Museum in Onchiota, New York. Over the years, I practically memorized the words on that recording.

What was Ray's message? We've misunderstood so much.

Vibrant cultures from all over the world have made our modern civilization what it is today. It's like a stew made up of many things from many cultures. Even though the Western Hemisphere likely contributed most of the ingredients to that stew, the contributions go unrecognized.

I couldn't tolerate how we have misunderstood history for such a long time. What my grandparents were taught bothered me. What my parents were taught bothered me. What I was taught bothered me. What kids are learning today bothers me. Our education hasn't changed much over the years.

As time went by, I dug more and more into my subject. I studied and read and learned and did extensive research. The world had changed for me. I came to this conclusion: What if Europeans and Indians were peers and co-equals, but then everybody forgot?

Then one day I couldn't stand the misinformation any longer. I had to do something about it myself. I reasoned, if this sudden change could happen to me, it could happen to others. So I thought, let's give it a try. Let's spread the message.

As a professional speaker, my job is to educate people. I Dispel the Lies of 1492. I inspire and educate my audiences by retelling actual histories so listeners realize Europeans and Indians were peers and co-equals – but then people forgot. History forgot.

The real-life facts are compelling and paint a different story than many of us know. Throughout this book, I detail how the Western Hemisphere truly functioned in 1492. Come along with me as I delve into the major activities of the Indians in the Western Hemisphere, including their advancements in government, technology, food, and health. While I can't go into everything, I cover many accomplishments such as the first democracy, their development of a predominantly stone transportation system consisting of 225,000 kilometres (140,000 mi.) of roadway, their knowledge of farming and crops making up 75% of our world's foods, women's rights, their construction of over 1,000 pyramids, their large populations and widespread coverage of the land, and their large cities.

We as a society continue to hide this fascinating information and make it invisible. Instead, we should be deconstructing the lies and creating the truth. We Westerners are wracked with guilt every time we hear something in the news about the Indigenous, past and present. Instead, we should do what we can to dispel the lies and become free of the guilt.

Because little of the true past is on our radar, I encourage people to look at their own circumstances today and recognize the extraordinary number of gifts the Native Indians gave the world. We love our way of life, and I challenge my readers to go out and transform their worldviews and attitudes. I give you a path to feel better with less guilt and to experience personal truth and reconciliation.

I'm really moved when someone tells me they changed their outlook, or when they tell me they're excited to share some of these details with others. I'm hoping you'll join that list. I want to reach as many people with my message and Dispel the Lies of 1492. I invite you to dive into this exciting topic with me.

When we increase our understanding, don't we feel better than when we were ignorant? It's true, the subjects surrounding Columbus and 1492 can be touchy. Going into further detail around the 500 years since then can also trigger heightened sensitivity. Indigenous issues are in the news constantly, and there can be some guilt by association.

The fear of guilt is partly what makes a lot of this information invisible to us, but if we can find a way past that fear, we'll feel a little better.

We'll feel better with understanding versus ignorance. We'll feel better because we have found a way past the fear of guilt by association.

Please note: What you read in the following pages is not a history book. If you're looking here for that type of lesson, you won't find it. To the source-hungry reader, I can only refer you to the Afterword.

SECTION 1

LIES *and* TRUTH

Exposed to delightful enriching histories, I was challenged to wonder, "what if almost every single part of your world is turning out to be based on lies?"

That query wasn't laid out quite that specifically or quite that obviously. It was simply placed within view. The question was constructed block by block in the way epiphanies often are. Many of the life-changing ideas in our individual histories are not discovered when a light is shone on some new knowledge. Human nature doesn't operate comfortably in that type of zone where information comes from outside and someone is telling us. With transformation, the obvious doesn't work as well as the fortuitous. We prefer our own ideas to those of others.

But as in Napoleon Hill's suggestion, when the truth is placed strategically to allow someone to conveniently *discover* it, that is when a life can be changed. That is when a worldview can truly be altered.

Unfortunately, the messages contained herein break this success rule by trying to push ideas through rather than casually leaving them in view to be suddenly embraced during a eureka moment. That luxury of casualness seems unavailable.

The much riskier method of pushing the ideas through grows from impatience and anger. It's taking too long to complete some of the basic repairs needed in our society. Let's get on with it.

≋ CHAPTER 1 ≋

Europeans and Indians Were Peers and Co-Equals, But Then People Forgot

I want to begin with some fundamentals about the premise, "all Europeans and Indians were co-equals, but then people forgot." In looking at these two groups, let's go back to 1492 and create a portrait of the world's OTHER land mass.

Note: Use of the term "Western Hemisphere" references South America, Mesoamerica, which is Central America, as well as North America, and the West Indies. The Western Hemisphere refers to all of those areas. When we speak about what existed in 1492, or what had been accomplished up until that time, the term Indians is simply referring to the Indigenous people of all those combined areas. The term Indians, along with many other imperfect terms describing these Indigenous peoples, although not always fashionable, is used intentionally and in a well researched way. I am well aware of the shortcomings of each term and of the inadmissibility of *any* term. (Indians themselves would prefer the correct actual tribal names of each of the 3,500 individual groups and in the proper language.)

Setting the Stage

By conducting a bit of an overview of the planet, we see Europe's population at 70 to 80 million around the year 1500. The Western Hemisphere's ever-increasing population estimates have settled in at more than 100 million people, although you may see estimates ranging from 65 million to as many as 145 million.

We are normally taught the land was pretty much empty and there was a lot of pristine wilderness on these continents except for a bunch of savages running around in diapers. This comfortable view has settled in over many, many, many generations and it's a view put there on purpose. Most people educated in our Western civilization are surprised the population of the two continents surpassed that of Europe prior to Columbus. Because of those large populations, explorer parties were typically met within minutes of their arrival on the shores of these lands.

The largest city in Europe at that time was Paris with a population of about 200,000 people. The largest city in the Western Hemisphere was Tenochtitlan, which was outside what is known as today's Mexico City. The population of Tenochtitlan was about 250,000 to 300,000 people. It was considered to be the most densely populated place on earth in 1492. The inhabitants lived in adobe dwellings.

In North America's southwest and in Mesoamerica, the world's first apartment complexes were these adobe dwellings. We know this from excavations where sites may have started off with 40, 50, or 60 units or dwellings. Over time, these com-

Spain funded the first trip to the Americas. Spain had been at war for 800 years...

munities were further developed by adding more families. Four hundred, 600, or 800 of these attached units could eventually make up the entire set of homes. The dwellings were very similar to today's apartment complexes reaching to a height of four stories at times.

These two distinct regions of the world met when Europeans began exploring the world. Spain funded the first trip to the Americas. Spain had been at war for 800 years, being ruled during much of that time by the Moors, a very dark-skinned people from the south. Now, we can pretty much surmise the impact of being at war for six years in the twentieth century, in today's civilization. Trying to picture being at war for a generation or so, 25 years let's say, that's difficult; but trying to imagine 800 years at war is impossible. It's a long time to be at war and certainly can change a culture beyond a point of reasonable analysis.

Health and Nutrition of Europeans
Let's look at Europe in 1492. During that time, the Europeans were not doing well. They were near the end of a period called the Dark Ages. The people were not healthy. Epidemics occurring from disease were common.

All of the countries in Europe were run by kings and queens and the noble system. They were 100% dictatorships. Of course, they had the nobles and dukes and barons and earls underneath the kings and queens. Many people within the rest of the population were eking out an existence. There were a lot of diseases. As many as 22 different diseases could sweep through in waves. These epidemics wiped out significant percentages of the population.

Let's quickly take a look at why disease in Europe was so rampant. Europeans had two strikes against them when it came to battling disease and the spread of disease: nutrition and hygiene.

Maintaining a nutritious diet was difficult in Europe. Barley, wheat, and rye did not have great yields, and even though there was some domestication of animals, livestock was not always a reliable source of nutrition. Consequently, there were a lot of poor people, and a lot of serfs, who were little better than slaves.

Unlike Europe, people in all areas of the Americas had very nutritious diets. Of course, no one knew about nutrition at that time, or the science of nutrition as we think of it, but they had balanced diets throughout the Americas. As we will delve into later, Indian civilizations were particularly advanced in all areas of food technology.

During this time in history, the Europeans lacked knowledge of the benefits of personal cleanliness and hygiene. They didn't bathe much because it was considered unhealthy. Queen Isabella, who sent Columbus to the Americas, bragged about bathing twice in her entire life – once when she was born and once when she was married. It was like a badge of honour. Queen Elizabeth I of England was very much the same; she was known to bathe only several times over a period of years.

Many people bathed a few times in their entire life. Having a bath was believed to be a source of sickness so they tried not to do it, or they did it sparingly. They thought the water could go inside different orifices of your body and was the cause of sickness. The idea was also backed up by the church because nakedness was frowned upon and was associated closely with sinful behaviour.

Several diseases were spread as a result of these unhygienic behaviours. Poor hygiene, when combined with poor nutrition, resulted in about 10% of the population being infirm or handicapped in some way, whether hunchbacked, lame, crippled, dumb, deaf, blind, or just plain insane. One out of every ten people had these types of afflictions.

Class systems

It's interesting to note class dominated everything in 1492, not just in Europe, but in most parts of the world ultimately influencing events in history. Today, race is on our radar all the time, but race being on our radar is really an outgrowth of class, and an end result of 500 years of compounded class system conditioning.

When people have been associated with a certain class for a long time, the viewpoints really convert themselves and become race associations or race issues. The visual context has sort of taken over, but at that time race was not an issue in this way. It was all related to class. You didn't go outside your class or even consider it. People were very conditioned to stay within their class. The class systems were deeply entrenched in society, and the behaviours expected of members in each class were rooted in the people.

In simplified terms, there are four main peoples in the world. We know they have *all* contributed equally to today's modern civilization: Asians, Africans, Caucasians, and the Indians of the Western Hemisphere. When these peoples met each other, or when different cultures and subcultures around the world met each other, class was the dominating force during the interactions. Commonly, nobility would attempt to associate with the nobility of the culture they were meeting. The people who were at the lower echelons, in terms of the class of a society, would also associate with those in the lower echelons of the other peoples' social framework.

It was also common for noble and powerful people to try to marry their sons and daughters immediately into the families of the culture they were interacting with as a way to solidify the relationship and strengthen their position. The Black, White, Asian, and Indian aspects were just not as significant as the class issues. They didn't notice that type of thing the way we do today. They weren't looking at everyone and asking "was this person Black or White." Race was not a defining part of the world in 1492.

In many of the North American cultures there was a sense of equilibrium in their social structures. They did not have pronounced classes in many societies. It was also considered a sin for anybody to go hungry. Even your worst enemy or your prisoners would not go hungry unless everybody went hungry. It was considered a shame to do something like that and was also fairly universal up and down all the different civilizations of the Western Hemisphere.

There's a story about a North American Indian in a European city becoming confused because of class issues. This individual, after visiting the huge mansion and estate, went out walking and within a few blocks noticed a lot of people starving and dying of starvation. He could not understand why there were people dying of starvation so close to this prominent estate.

First of all, why didn't the hungry have the food, and why were they not given the food? Second, why wouldn't they just strangle the people who had all the food, or perhaps burn their houses down, or find some other solution? This man couldn't figure this out because he didn't understand the rigidity of the class system.

The nobility had the military might, but that was not the issue at stake. The people in the lower classes wouldn't consider such rebellious acts. It just wouldn't be done. The members of European society were firmly entrenched into their classes and it ruled their behaviour. The Indian was confused because the civilizations were so different from one another.

Territories, language, and culture

In the Western Hemisphere, we're looking at about 3,500 distinct jurisdictions. There are different terms for these: nations, communities, bands, countries, pueblos, districts, provinces, municipalities, civilizations, territories, tribes, towns, lands, states, regions, areas, villages, and cities. In almost all cases, area residents had a complete awareness of their territorial boundaries. They knew their region and they knew where it ended. They had imaginary lines, just as we do today. Rivers, trails, and landmarks served as boundaries just like everywhere else in the world. But the land was certainly taken. It was accounted for; the old cliché idea that Indigenous peoples up and down the Americas didn't own territory is just not true.

There is some truth in the widely held view regarding lack of individual property rights in many parts of the Americas.

...the land was certainly taken. It was accounted for...

Land was often considered sacred and not even subject to "ownership." This contrasts with the nobility systems of every European region, where kings and queens with the divine right of the church cordoned off the continent in a complex legal framework of direct ownership.

However, the Indigenous peoples did have ownership in terms of their overall territory. National groups and tribal communities knew their boundaries very well. Unlike a common faulty worldview, it wasn't a lot of pristine wilderness just waiting for somebody to move in and occupy it. That lie has been purposely planted and nurtured and kept alive.

Ironically, in some North American Indigenous settlements which became 100% depopulated, mostly through disease, Europeans did actually move into the empty towns.

So there was an unknown number of distinct territories; around 3,500. There were thousands of languages. The exact number is not known, but we can agree there were thousands of distinct languages and certainly a lot of rich cultures. Each of these areas' civilizations made huge impacts on their natural environments and shared habits of transforming ecologies on a continent-wide scale.

For instance, in South America, residents in the Andes did a lot with textiles and fibres. They had healthy, balanced diets and developed an astonishing array of food plants. The inhabitants of Mesoamerica, which includes parts of Mexico, the Yucatán, and parts of Central America, were also magnificent farmers known for giving corn to the world. They are without a doubt the world leaders in pyramids and pyramid-based cultures. North America was known for their pyramid mounds, irrigation projects, rich farming, and classless social structures.

In North America, war was not practiced in a way we would consider warfare by today's standards or by European standards at the time. They were more like skirmishes, almost closer to a sport. When they went to war they didn't all line up to kill each other. Their styles of warfare could be more accurately described not as battles, but as guerilla-style skirmishes.

Trade went on everywhere throughout the Indigenous territories, and since Mesoamerica was near the middle of the hemisphere, they were very influential when it came to trading. Trading habits and routes were being established around 5000 BC. Widespread trade was well established by 3000 BC, including transfers of goods between the South American areas and the North American areas. As an example, corn was found all the way up north as far as it could be grown and was found south into South America as far as it could be grown. So corn covered most of these two continents.

Population loss

OK, let's have some more statistics. Let's look at the 140-year period between 1500 and 1640. It is now understood in 140 years, one out of every five people on earth perished in Indian epidemics. In other words, disease that spread through the Indian population took the lives of 20% of the population of the earth. It is the greatest loss of life, demographically, in human history. We're talking about some large populations along with some major effects when these diseases swept through the Americas.

Diseases had been sweeping through Europe at random intervals for centuries. We are aware of those dates throughout history when certain diseases came and the same applies to the Western Hemisphere. Historians know which dates certain diseases hit and roughly what level of decimation they caused.

Indians from the Western Hemisphere can be treated as a contiguous group. There are so many close associations in their health practices, common medicines, and particularly the foods they ate such as the corn, beans, and squash example that had spread throughout most of the hemisphere. That type of sharing and trade is what leads into the contiguous side, commenting on them as one people.

However, just as the peoples of Eurasia and Africa shared goods on the one hand while being extremely diverse on the other, Indians showed wide variations in cultural direction. Therefore, Indians can also be depicted as quite distinct from one another in 1492.

This can be shown by the South American and Mesoamerican practices of either slavery or class differences, along with the often brutal autocratic systems of government. North America historically had much more voluntary systems of government, and the Iroquois, a subset passion of mine, gave us the system of governance many are trying to spread around the world today.

We will be looking into the combined accomplishments of these continents' residents. Whether we view them as one of four "races" of the world, or whether we choose to explore the astonishingly diverse achievements among the groups, population loss always prevails as a common thread. It is the differentia of their story.

≋ CHAPTER 2 ≋

When Children Find Out What We Did

In preparation for the numerous fascinating accounts of these two continents prior to 1492, let's consider the vantage point of you, the reader. It's possible you currently see a world in which very little of importance took place in the Western Hemisphere. When you are exposed to the astonishing new accounts of the past, is your viewpoint subject to change? Are you capable of altering your paradigms?

Today, it's well understood how difficult it is to alter our own beliefs. Our bodies are designed to filter out information that does not fit our existing belief system. Discomfort caused by new data from our senses can be interpreted as threatening and, in many cases, fail to even reach the destination in our cerebrums. Sadly, penetrating our own defences is not completely within our control.

What if the happiness of your children or grandchildren depended on you and your view?

Harsh messages for children

White folks everywhere have considered this whole world to be their civilization. They thought all this up themselves across the ocean. It's been important to teach our children everything good and great must have come from the White man's land, Europe.

In concentrating on gifts and contributions, thousands of heart-wrenching histories and anecdotes are missing within these pages. To embark upon scouring these is to set you up for heartbreak. Most stories of Western Hemisphere cultural encounters start out bad and continue to get worse and worse. Many of the true historical books are just too disturbing to read through to the end.

Prepare first the little Caucasian girls and boys. What words could be said to our children to bring them into the twenty-first century to harden them to the harshness of some of the messages?

A quick Google search for "Wikipedia genocide of Indigenous peoples" will take you on a rapid journey around the world as you scan through over 30 categories, starting with the Western Hemisphere. This will not be an uplifting part of your day, but it becomes plain this complex word is no longer forbidden. For children today, the word genocide is moving from the internet into their mainstream education.

And a genocide that goes on and on and on for 500 years is so confusing for everybody. The term really refers to the decimation of any population, in this case Indians, down to 5% or 10% of what it used to be. Europeans managed to achieve zero percent by completely erasing some cultures, but how simplified things would be if that pesky 5% wasn't around.

Much like war, genocide is messy and chaotic and uncertain. It's a 500-year war. A war on happiness against a race called the American Indian. It's a war on truth. It's a war on correctness. It's a war on accurate information. It's a war on the minds of little children having to grow up ashamed for so many innumerable generations. Even the strongest cultures repeatedly crack under a strain like this.

It's true, the genocide **you** took part in was partly accidental. But no one tends to accept full responsibility for genocide anyway, do they? [Well, some do.]

Countless missionaries and governments have worked to try to make Indian children feel ashamed of their heritage. When you make someone ashamed of their own grandfathers and grandmothers, you've used a tactic that does the worst possible damage to a little person's mind. The person is lost; probably forever.

If you feel you are successfully detaching yourself from the events of 400 and 500 years ago, check with those kids today who might say to you, "How could they have done that?" or "How could *we* have done that?" or even "How could *you* have done that?" Children don't have as much conditioning as we do when it comes to hardening themselves against taking any responsibility for shameful events of the past. They have grown up with the "we thought all this up over there across the ocean" paradigm and have been taught to take credit for the feel-good side of history.

...a genocide that goes on and on and on for 500 years is so confusing for everybody.

On one hand, "we thought all this up over there." On the other hand, "all this bad stuff from hundreds of years ago has nothing to do with me." How do we manage to put off and avoid reconciling these two thoughts? It takes some cultural gymnastics, some intellectual hoop jumping, and some conscience-sedating techniques to fit this comfortably into a worldview. It's learned slowly over time, as we grow up.

What if today's global youngsters are missing some of the hard-wired acceptance of everything they're told? Truth seeking is creeping into the world's psyche. Events involving twentieth century natives, numerous and scandalous, are dominating the news. Indigenous issues are landing in classrooms everywhere. Psychologists are being called in to advise teachers on handling these delicate subjects. Educators are being instructed on how to end these classes, lest students arrive at home traumatized. To make matters worse for these youngsters, this is only one of many challenges facing them now and in the future.

Playing both sides of the history game has worked for several generations, but now the house of cards is beginning to fall apart. On the one hand, White children are taught to be proud of their heritage; on the other hand, they are told to distance themselves from any shameful legacy.

New generations of youngsters want to peek past the confusion, and they haven't even yet learned some of the Indian gifts to the world kids use today: chewing gum, vanilla, peanuts, popcorn, potato chips, chocolate, caramel corn, maple syrup, french fries, bouncing balls, toothbrushes and toothpaste, kites, stilts, and balloons.

Once you learn about some of the gifts Indians gave to us you can see the fog begin to lift. A landscape of truth might be allowed to emerge. Prepare for a long, slow transition to a new understanding. Prepare for two generations of shifting thoughts and altered images. Prepare to meet a new and wonderful people who have made many unrecognized contributions to our civilization. Prepare to be fascinated by a story so much more compelling than the garbage fed to the world about the Americas' Indians, and I mean just that – garbage.

The fog is beginning to lift.

It's everybody's civilization

In the past, we might typically refer to our "White man's civilization." What is the White man's civilization? Have you ever stopped to consider it? Whose civilization is this? The White man is taking a lot of credit for something that doesn't rightfully belong to him. White men didn't invent reading. They didn't invent writing. They didn't invent arithmetic. Those three important contributions were made by a very dark-skinned people thousands of miles to the south of Europe. They then spread north to Greece and Europe.

We can all say "this is **our** civilization," but no one race or peoples has a right to say "this is my civilization." Every race has made great contributions to our civilization and in equal amounts, but I want to look at the American Indian race. Everything we have been exposed to makes it very easy to picture Indians as a bunch of savages running around out in the woods

The White man is taking a lot of credit for something that doesn't rightfully belong to him.

with diapers on, but that viewpoint is wholly incorrect. The American Indians have had shame indoctrinated into them for countless generations. It hasn't been completely successful because they have a lot to be proud of today.

The Indians/Natives of the Western Hemisphere gave gifts to the world that were as varied as they were. They had many civilizations, both ancient and modern. They had thousands of languages. They were always a welcoming people, up and down 30,000 km (18,000 mi.) of coastline. What they had they gave freely to the European visitors.

But the intent of all Europeans along that American coastline was the same: conquest. It was the original plan, and it has been relentlessly carried out over 500 years. Every attempt to help the Indigenous has been clouded by Euro-blindness. Uncle Sam and Uncle Ottawa and 35 modern governments have turned their backs on Indians in a repeating pattern. Whites have also continually turned their backs on their own pledges, their own integrity, and their own religious teachings.

I want to present to you a paradox about a misguided attempt at integrity by our mainstream conquering societies. The history books are full of lies and omissions because the truth is not a proud story for Caucasians. They have been attempting to uphold the myths and, therefore, retain a sense of integrity along the way. Yet when the upholding of these fabrications is no longer possible, the truth will finally become everyday knowledge. The White man's lack of integrity will eventually be discovered. The lies were constructed to avoid shame, but when the truth is revealed, even more intensified feelings of shame could result. Those are the contradictory features of these colonial histories.

Whites have used brutal tactics during their takeovers. Before finishing the long campaign, they practically conquered the whole world. IF THEY'RE DONE YET!

Let me submit a hypothesis: we are still waging a war on all little children who are kept in the dark about some shameful activities in the past. Now the truth is poised to begin tumbling out into the mainstream of our society. Can little Caucasian children withstand that? Yes; a simple yes.

Our children are ready to stand up and become real citizens of the world instead of the pretend people their ancestors have been. Their ancestors failed to grasp the truth from behind the walls of gated communities. The true stories of the Western Hemisphere are far more fascinating than the silly fairy stories we have been producing and believing.

The White man has been riding high ever since Pizarro looked down from his horse at the natives he was slaughtering. Whites can afford to come down a notch or two. Psychologically, they will come out no less damaged than their current state. We can survive it easily. If the Indigenous can do it, we can do it. Join a new movement of people who are feeling proud on their behalf. Internalize the truth. Then share it. Spread it around.

Disease

Children and adults alike might be surprised at some of the injustices of the past, whether they are advertent or inadvertent. As history unfolded, disease played a huge, but accidental, role in every regional story without exception. Large populations were lost as European diseases affected the health of the Indigenous. Let us be sure the reader is aware diseases did *not* travel the other way. The Indians did not spread any disease to the European visitors.

To properly unpack its implications, I need to become technical here as I cover the disease aspect.

One of the most important inventions in Europe, the printing press, created an interesting phenomenon. For a little background, the printing press was invented in 1450. Before then, books had been a complete rarity. Then the printing press came along, and by the time 50 or 100 years went by people were enjoying this new freedom. They loved publications. The information from the New World went back to Europe where they were captivated by books and reading and especially fascinated with Indian stories.

A foundational fact is Europeans during colonization were meeting a lot of peoples, civilizations, states, territories, towns, and villages **already** decimated and depopulated due to disease. The diseases spread inland very quickly. In turn, reports going back to Europe during the time would quite often be reports from someone meeting Indians in areas recently hit with disease and depopulated.

It has been realized only recently the extreme quickness with which the diseases spread. In most cases, the disease had already hit towns and villages *before* the Europeans even arrived in the villages because of the volume of trade occurring and the rapidness of the transmission. This fact has had a big impact on history.

These reports and their ramifications have been called Holmberg's Mistake by Charles Mann, who outlines the flawed research of anthropologist, Allan Holmberg, in one twentieth century example. The Sirionó people lost 95% of their population due to disease. Although a caring and careful companion to the Sirionó tribespeople of South America, the scientist failed to grasp the truth about their condition, or why they appeared to be so primitive. His 1950 writings of their way of life became so influential they helped create the permanent incorrect image of South America's Indigenous which persists to this day. The phenomenon of Holmberg's Mistake went on all the way down through the centuries; in the 1500s, 1600s, 1700s, 1800s, and right up into the 1900s.

So on to the next aspect of diseases and more technicalities. The immunization spectrum of the Western Hemisphere inhabitant was very, very narrow. Immunization spectrum refers to the vulnerability of any group when considering how similar one person is compared to the next person. How similar is one person's immune system compared to another person's?

We know from the DNA of the Indigenous populations of the Western Hemisphere their immunization spectrum is very narrow compared to anyone else on earth. It relates to the ancient history of Proto-Indians. We don't know for sure, yet, if they entered the hemisphere, how they entered, how many times they may have entered, and why they have these narrow immunization spectrums, but their susceptibility to disease factored into world history.

The lack of immunization spectrum in the Indian population had a great effect on their culture after their introduction to the Europeans. Wherever Europeans went on these two continents the result was always disappearing civilizations. There were no exceptions.

For example, let's take a look at the black plague. When a major epidemic swept through Europe, a 30% death toll would be considered high. Forty to 60% would be among the worst ever. In the Americas, the common death rate was 80% to 90%, and in some cases the death toll could reach 100%.

A 95% mortality rate was common enough because there were many examples of Europeans going in and visiting a town that had been depopulated to 5% of the previous population 5 or 10 or 20 years before.

Let's first picture a series of towns which lost 95% of their people to smallpox, and then let us add 20 years to the picture. What would we find? We can guess we would fine deteriorated infrastructure, no sense of cultural or community intelligence, continuing recovery from a period of subsistence or famine, lower levels of hunting and food production, untaught young people who grew up as small children fending for themselves, neighbouring villages perhaps fighting over scarce resources, forced alliances, poor health, and lingering mood of grief.

So, you can picture what kind of inaccurate reports were going back to the person's superiors and back to European society. The image of the American Indian has been destroyed, even though they had so much; for instance, antiseptics, brain surgery, and dental implants. Some had discovered electricity, figured out electroplating and were using it. Our hosts on these two continents were not backward at all and had so many advancements. But that information has all been lost within our common, day-to-day lives, and it has been a convenient loss for the European conquerors. These stone-age tribespeople fallacies have a lot to do with why we are still stuck with wildly inaccurate ideas about Indians.

In today's civilizations we can change our view of these cultures as we simultaneously change our view about what happened. These "kids finding out what we did" will become adults and realize the brutality was accompanied by some coincidence, some benign behaviours, and some luck favouring the conquest-oriented Europeans.

We see a blend of willful holocaust and inadvertent catastrophe. On the side of chance, the bubonic plague, tetanus, typhoid, malaria, yellow fever, measles, mumps, encephalitis, tuberculosis, smallpox, influenza, whooping cough, dysentery, cholera, typhus, diphtheria, scarlet fever, pleurisy, venereal disease, common cold, rabies, and goiter.

A whopping list and all could be deadly.

When researchers look at the records from many of the explorers, from Columbus, and from the Indigenous themselves, they must read into disease descriptions to try and figure out which diseases they, in fact, were.

In the twenty-first century, we look at many things through a scientific lens, and assume history had today's terminology. In the same way as people in 1492 had no scientific terms surrounding nutrition, they had no words for the diseases they encountered, not like we do today. Records show diseases were

These stone-age tribespeople fallacies have a lot to do with why we are still stuck with wildly inaccurate ideas about Indians.

typically described in the 1400s or 1500s as the shakes, sores, fever, spots, fevers with shakes, fevers with spots and a lot of shakes and open sores with tiredness; these types of descriptions. Organized naming systems for diseases didn't exist as yet.

All 22 diseases impacted the world. Let's examine some details surrounding malaria, an ailment consisting of two distinct types. Malaria #2 has played its large part in world history mainly because it remains within a person's bloodstream for decades. It could affect people suddenly and randomly causing them to become too tired to even do anything. The symptom could last for six months. It might also sweep through a town or village when some inhabitants had, in fact, been infected 15 years earlier.

Not only did malaria act as this never-ending wild card in American relationships, it even indirectly caused the demographic makeup of later populations. As early encounters wiped out Indigenous peoples, Europeans came to realize they were killing off their own workforce of slaves. Since Africans' exposure to malaria in childhood gave them immunity, African slaves were transported to the Americas in huge numbers.

Twelve to 14 million Africans slaves were transported to the newly discovered hemisphere in the 300 years between 1500 and 1800. Only one out of six survived the unspeakable ordeal from hometown to coast to ship to final destination. Let us remember those 60 to 70 million dead Africans when we debate the body count resulting from White colonialism.

What did the populations of the Americas look like after 300 years? Indian records on all subjects were largely destroyed or made illegal, whether one is considering artifact-based items or oral histories being disrupted. So figures are never certain. The natives had suffered massive loss of life, but were still the most common ingredient to the mix of peoples in the numerous colonial-dominated areas. Twelve to 14 million Blacks had been brought to these continents. Only 3 million to 4 million Europeans lived here, even at the late date of 1800. Europeans were normally not immune to malaria and over the centuries many were fearful of travel to the Americas.

Europeans were dominating politically and culturally, but still remained a minority due to the ever-prevalent disease factor. So when considering the most common images from the 1600s and 1700s, think of native Indigenous and Blacks interacting together with Whites being a background feature in the visible day-to-day lives of the average inhabitants.

Yes, children will find a jumble of chaotic images when they embark on these discoveries, when they set out to make an orderly set of chronicles for their developing minds. But unknowns are still superior to lies, and they're worth building upon.

The truth about disease is a critical part of facing up to what happened in South and North America; substantial pre-existing populations, massive loss of life, devastation of countless cultural communities and civilizations, and the one-way-only travel nature of the disease turmoil.

In the Western Hemisphere, without livestock available, families did not live in close quarters with animals. The European home technology was on par with that of the Western

Hemisphere. But in Europe and elsewhere in the world, it was common to have humans and animals housed together in their barn-like homes. This existed for thousands of years in Europe, Asia, and Africa.

Thus, many of Europe's deadliest diseases were animal illnesses that had jumped the species barrier. Cows spread measles and tuberculosis, chickens transferred influenza and whooping cough, and horses transported encephalitis and smallpox.

We now know what Holmberg did not know. Our children can now know what Holmberg did not know. We share Western countries with Indigenous of countless varieties. But, like Holmberg, we fail to grasp the most basic information forming their story. We misinterpret even when we are trying to help.

In summary, the immunization spectrum has combined with disease travelling inland so quickly, which has, in turn, combined with these reports going back to Europe. Together, it has made the situation with the diseases even more tragic than it would have been with just the massive loss of life.

SECTION 2

The EXTRAORDINARY NUMBER *of* NATIVE INDIAN GIFTS *to the* WORLD

In these pages, I provide a small sampling of the many interesting stories to be told regarding the accomplishments, innovations, and inventions of the native populations of the Western Hemisphere. The full collection is formidable and full of ideas that have transferred around the world. Invention stories contain their own intrigue, detail, and richness, and only a few can be covered here. Many of these innovations may have belonged to one civilization, or may have existed within one time period; therefore, one cannot read into this and assume all societies had a such and such way of life, the way we do today. There is an ebb and flow to the introduction and spreading of new ways.

We can picture world civilization as if it's rolling out over a period of centuries and millennia with fits and starts thrown into the mix. In this slice of world civilization we look into, if it seems to you the Europeans are herein depicted with a harsh light, you would be correct. However, remember the image of the Indian of the Americas has been destroyed over time. Their shattered image is a prevalent problem throughout the world, across all cultures, and across all heritage types.

Even though there are only so many narratives I can share here, a variety of them are highlighted. Throughout this section I share some of my favourite Native Indian contributions. I fail to understand why much of this information isn't easily available, and it's a shame we have not provided these fascinating details to kids. I do not want today's generation to reach a similar abrupt, unanticipated conclusion as I did, while sitting listening to a radio show in my car. By sharing some of the Native Indians' gifts to the world, we can begin to work towards uncovering the truth.

◆ CHAPTER 3 ◆

Government

Let's look at gifts of ideas and thought and governance. That's my favourite section, involving our Northern Indians and the Iroquois Confederacy.

Iroquois Confederacy

I'll begin with the Iroquois, who refer to themselves as Haudenosaunee, meaning Longhouse People. They lived in bark houses called longhouses. Those homes were known to Europeans to be more airtight and more waterproof than the European wattle-and-daub houses, as they're called. Europeans often commented in their many records that native homes were not drafty like European homes. There have been excavated sites of longhouses over 450 feet long and 50 feet across. It's certainly no little shack, but a good-sized building.

Founded in 1142, the Iroquois Confederacy was the world's first United Nations, designed to do away with war. It combined five nations together into the Iroquois Confederacy. The Great Peacemaker was a visitor from the north who instigated and helped initiate the Iroquois Confederacy. He was a remarkable influence, setting in motion a system and society with remarkable features. For instance, they had a constitution, which is still operating today.

About 60 or 70 years ago, modern historians finally began to admit the American Constitution was borrowed and imprinted directly from the Iroquois Constitution. Congress made this very clear when the U.S. House of Representatives passed House Concurrent Resolution 331 (H.Con.Res. 331) in 1988. There are about 25 similarities between the two systems, and there are some key differences.

The similarities between the Iroquois and American Constitutions make sense when you understand the Europeans and Indians lived closely together. Thomas Jefferson, George Washington, Benjamin Franklin, and many others all knew the Iroquois very well. They dealt with them in an administrative capacity. The Iroquois had often urged them to combine the colonies together so the Indians and settlers could deal with issues in an organized way.

The Iroquois were organized, and they were strong. When the population of the colonies eventually came to outnumber the Indigenous 50 to 1, settlers still begged the Iroquois for protection, and they received it.

This type of government was nothing like the monarchies in Europe. This governmental arrangement that had been formulated in ancient times was based on equal representation and the election of leaders through a nominating system. Colonists knew of the Iroquois system, and they were aware of it all over Europe, as well. Monarchies sent spies over to see about it, and to check out this very "dangerous" framework of laws where the people chose their own leaders.

Under the noble systems in place everywhere in Europe at the time, the monarch ruled no matter what. The people might have hated them. The ruler may have been cruel or incompetent. In some cases, they were insane, and everyone knew they were insane. But it made no difference. They ruled no matter what, and their oldest sons or daughters took over no matter what. The system was supported by every one of their Christian religions.

European leaders knew the election system was not good for them. They were afraid of it and with good reason. Eventually, it rubbed off on the Americans. Beyond the election of leaders, the two constitutions have a very similar setup, with the two houses voting separately, along with the checks and balances built into the law-making format.

During the first 12 years of the United States of America, the Articles of Confederation attempted to follow the unanimous voting system the Iroquois had enjoyed for hundreds of years. Reaching a full consensus was a very common widespread Indigenous formality. In the Iroquois constitution, a bill had to be unanimous to pass. But it is well documented that because the colonies had so many disagreements about the land they were stealing, they changed to today's majority system.

The Iroquois Confederacy's concept led the way from another important standpoint, besides the United Nations aspect. It was also the world's first real democracy.

Now, we have all been taught everything good and great had to come from the land of kings and queens across the ocean, and people will look with a magnifying glass all over

The Iroquois Confederacy's concept led the way from another important standpoint, besides the United Nations aspect. It was also the world's first real democracy.

Europe vainly and desperately for an example of democracy. They'll come up with the answer; the Greeks had a democracy. We have all been educated about Greek democracy, haven't we?

Did the Greeks have a democracy? Let's take a look at this claim. First, the majority of the Greeks were slaves. Any country with slavery is not a real democracy. Second, all the women were owned. They were chattel or property. Third, the elderly had no say; young people had no say.

In the Iroquois Confederacy everybody had a say; everybody had a voice. This is real democracy. Even young people at the age of reason had a say. The age of reason meant 14 or 15 years old.

Children's rights still don't exist today in Western civilization; they haven't really entered into our awareness. It would make sense by now any person at the age of reason who wished to take part in society would be given the opportunity to have a voice, a say, but we have yet to aspire to the level of equality found in the Iroquois system.

The biggest difference with the Iroquois is the fact they are a matrilineal society, and the women have always had equal rights. Some would even contend the society functioned as a matriarchate; a civil government supervised by women. Women only started voting in the 1900s in modern "democracies." In some places in Europe, women still weren't given the right to vote until the 70s, 80s, or 90s, but the Iroquois have always had this type of system in place. Simply put, they had a democracy.

The slave trade was a huge business all over the world; Africa, Lisbon, New England, and many different ports took part. Settler societies throughout the Americas were very involved with transporting slaves, and they moved slaves just as they moved other goods. But slaves ran away whenever possible. Runaway slaves were a huge liability for slave traders to the extent hundreds of secret off-the-grid slave towns were developed and created over the centuries. These "maroon" towns have played a part in modern history on both continents, and in most countries, including around 50 of them in the United States.

To reduce losses, slave traders and slave owners used the Indians for tracking down and returning runaways. However, slavery was completely outlawed in all the Iroquois territory and always was throughout their history. The Iroquois refused to take part in all activity related to the slave trade, thereby acting as a limiting influence for slave-trading activity in that part of North America. Later, the Mason-Dixon Line, which became such an important aspect of the Civil War, had a lot to do with the sphere of influence from the Iroquois Confederacy.

When we understand these differences, we now know democracy came not from the Greeks but from the Iroquois. When we take a look at this new definition of democratization we can see the United States was not a real democracy when it started either because not everyone had a voice in the government. Slavery was an integral part of society. George Washington and Thomas Jefferson both had over 450 slaves in their final estates, a small fortune in itself. Analysts today can still debate whether the twenty-first century United States offers everyone a voice; whether they manage to maintain a standard as high as the Haudenosaunee.

The Iroquois Confederacy played an important part in Colonial America. The English and French were asked to settle their mutual colonial disagreements and differences using the Iroquois system. The idea of the Iroquois Confederacy was to do away with war. They were not a warlike people as you have read in the history books. All peoples were asked to take refuge under the Tree of Peace and "bury the hatchet" while negotiating and settle their differences peacefully. Factions insisting on using force instead of settling their differences by counsel were always given three chances.

When the English and French were invited to settle their

issues by peaceful discussion and counsel under the Tree of Peace, they did not comprehend the Great Law or the Peacemaker's original message of harmony. The current administration told the Europeans to do any of their fighting on their own land across the ocean, if they could not settle and agree. But the Europeans had always settled their differences by blood and war. Just look at their history. Before they were finished, they practically conquered the whole world (are they even finished yet?)! We know they, too, were mostly fighting over the land they were stealing.

The Iroquois not only influenced democracy but the Iroquois Confederacy was also the basis or trigger for collectivist socialist thought and equality-based economies. They had equilibrium and equality built into the foundational constitution and ideas. Friedrich Engels was the one whose writing was the most famous for influencing people like Marx and Lenin, and he is known to have written his treatise "On the Origins of the Family, Private Property and the State" after he read Lewis Morgan's studies of the Iroquois.

Although the name Engels conjures up recollections of communist extremes in government, the ideas he presented were brand new and introduced as a flattening of the pyramidical dictator model of government. It offered an alternative. Those alternatives have evolved into many of the policies we associate with progressive modern governments such as protection of the poor, subsidies for the vulnerable, higher taxes for the wealthy, social security, pensions, temporary welfare support, maternity leaves, etc. All western democracies have some roots in the innovative concepts first explored by these political writers.

Many of the Iroquois practices were very strange to the Europeans. For example, on top of having no slavery, the Iroquois societies did not have equivalent words for sexual assaults, and had nothing equivalent to rape in their culture. At the time, all European societies had legalized marital rape and legalized wife beating. Some other practices the settlers took exception to include the freedom given to the native youngsters, the easy-going approach to childrearing, and the absence of corporal punishment with the children i.e., sparing the rod, or absence of child beating in today's parlance.

Women's rights are also directly tracked back to the Iroquois Confederacy and again this influence travelled all over the world. It's well documented how the early suffragettes were good friends with many Iroquois women and were influenced by them because Iroquois women basically ran their society. Women in England gained the right to vote just before World War I, and the United States shortly after World War I. Susan Anthony, Lucretia Mott, Matilda Gage, Lucy Stone, and Elizabeth Stanton were early suffragettes who paid homage to Iroquois women. Matilda Gage said, "Under Iroquois women the science of government reached the highest form known to the world." Even twenty-first century women today would find the rights of the female in Iroquois society to be unparalleled.

Iroquois women were the landowners and the farmers. In most Indian philosophies, women were the ones who gave life to humans, so they were, in turn, the ones in charge of giving life from the earth. I'll touch more on this in later pages but 75% of the foods grown in the world today were gifts from the

Women's rights are also directly tracked back to the Iroquois Confederacy and again this influence travelled all over the world.

American Indian. When we look at these provisions being cultivated on Indian farms, there were a lot of women developing foods on those farms.

Women nominated the chiefs and they could also have them kicked out of office. This is another thing that scared the people operating the noble systems in Europe. The Indians could actually remove someone from office, and the women played a large part in these decisions.

Our concepts of liberty and freedom came from our Northern Indians. These concepts are partly what fascinated Europeans when I spoke about their eagerness to read about Indians. These ideas disturbed the intellectual Europeans. They disturbed the monarchs and nobles who sent their spies to collect more details. They disturbed writers and thinkers. Philosophers such as Locke, Rousseau, and Thoreau were also fascinated by the Iroquois society and Indian thought. A lot of the writings and ideas of utopia that came into being were a direct or indirect result of Indian influences.

Montaigne in the 1500s hosted a Brazilian native. Locke in the 1600s impacted views regarding property rights after studying the differences between European and Iroquois cultures. Rousseau in the 1700s popularized the notion of the "common man," contrasting the noble system. Thoreau and Franklin, in the 1800s, both commented on the great oratorical skills of the Iroquois, because it was the ability to persuade others during law making that determined leadership, not being born into the ruling class. Benjamin Franklin said,

> "The Indian men, when young, are hunters and warriors, when old, counselors. For all their government is by counsel of the sages; there is no force, there are no prisons, no officers to compel obedience, or inflict punishment. Hence, they generally study the art of oratory speaking and the best speaker has the most influence."

There are layers and layers to the European adoption of Indian thought. The "noble Indian" and the "noble savage" were respected on the one hand, yet reviled on the other, amounting to a baffling mix of responses showing up in literature. It is clear that the "savage" people governing themselves without a king had an incalculable impact upon the great thinkers of these eras. Granted, Europe was in the midst of its own lie-producing machinery, accepting easy-to-digest explanations for the thievery and mayhem taking place across the ocean, yet still irresistibly drawn to the startling new ways of living revealed by the many accounts.

The wooden Indian beside the cigar store haunts us today. It represents a glimpse of a greater possibility for humanity, a people all living with a perpetual sense of freedom, not dominating others and in turn unable to be dominated, managing a complex society without jails or poor people or individual legal property rights. However, the wooden Indian also represents the inferior savage, the person unworthy of the wider equality controlled by the colonists, an object of scorn and pity. Myths and true stories blended together in the Euro-mindset, with ideas plucked where convenience served.

Courageous historians such as Arthur Parker and Paul Wallace are to be commended for starting to turn the tide around the middle of the twentieth century by shining some light of truth on Indigenous history. As Berkhofer observes,

"For most Whites throughout the past five centuries, the Indian of imagination and ideology has been as real [as], perhaps more real, than the Native American of actual existence and contact. As preconception became conception and conception became fact, the Indian was used for the ends of argument, art, and entertainment by White painters, philosophers, poets, novelists, and moviemakers among many."

Whites still don't know what to believe. It's complicated. Do you believe old stereotype claims about the North American freedom movement being a result of purely European invention? If so, and if we are to believe the English Magna Carta led to the US Constitution, isn't it strange a war was fought between them *over* the issue of representation? Read the Magna Carta searching for any mention of "the people," and you will find none. It is a reworking by the king, appeasing the nobility and allowing the nobles to renew the carving up of their personal ownership of the entire country.

Independence movements in Europe and beyond can be traced back to the Iroquois. The ideas of freedom and liberty spread to the Americas then spread to France with the French Revolution. It went on to England because the nobles and royalty there knew they were going to lose their heads the way the French nobles had lost their heads.

These virtues eventually spread all around the world and are still with us today. Let's take the example of the Arab Spring where people on the streets would spontaneously begin singing, "We Shall Overcome," a common American freedom song. When the Berlin Wall fell, similar types of "Americanisms" were brought out in the storylines. The sense of freedom and liberty is associated back to America and is directly attributable to the Iroquois system of government, along with the fiercely independent attitude of many of the North American Indians.

The land of kings and queens may still be with us today in our culture. Are we striving for equilibrium in our society or are we bound by thoughts from the 1400s? Do we all still dream of being kings and queens the way things have been for a thousand years?

The noble wanted to be the king and the people in the privileged classes wanted to be nobles. The people in the merchant class preferred to be privileged class, and the poor serfs were little better than slaves. They no doubt dreamt of the merchant class. Were these people dreaming about a world where everybody can have equilibrium, which is what some of these Indian societies had? No, I think they were dreaming about being the king and queen and having the ability to lord it over people.

Even slaves, after generations of conditioning, probably had the same dream of someday being able to lord it over others. Did the husband lord it over his wife, and the wife lord it over the children, leaving the children to wait until they grew up to experience the feeling? I think we're all still stuck in this paradigm today. I can't say we're working hard day to day to move ahead so someday we can have a society where we have equilibrium. I think we're trying to progress so we can lord it over someone else.

Let's do a quick check of what they did not have in the Iroquois Confederacy. They did not have rape, did not have seduction, and did not have child abuse of any kind, which Europeans commented on vocally and often. They did not have sexual abuse. There were no poor houses or jails. They didn't have theft or slavery. There was really no domination of others, and there was no gender inequality.

There was no mistreatment of prisoners. Those stories have all been debunked. They didn't even have a standing army, as most of the Europeans did. They had extremely capable militia and warriors were called in when something had to be resolved, but they did not have standing armies. Another debunked story is the one told about massacres where the victor kills innocent people, particularly women and children, at the end of a battle. There's not one accurate, true record of Indigenous Indians ever perpetrating massacres. Furthermore, they did not do any fighting off of their own land.

What type of society are we trying to create today? How are we thinking and governing ourselves today? The influences are easy to track. It is yet another example of the axiom. Our civilization is made of everyone's contributions, and Native Indians made more than their share to the good side.

Consider the Native Indians' contributions to our current civilization including those highlighted above: equal rights; the world's first true democracy; concepts of freedom and liberty; women's rights; children's rights; sustainable socialist ideas; and the first United Nations.

Is this sometimes cranky and cynical writer of "500 Years of Lies" bias toward the Iroquois? Perhaps, but it's not an unfair prejudice in their favour, is it? Probably displaying partiality? Yes. Enthusiastically wanting to share the convoluted place we have arrived politically? Yes. Remember, whenever you or your loved ones feel engaged with the bigger picture governing forces in your day-to-day lives dwell upon the mystery of the Iroquois, and how they were made invisible to us.

Political Examples

Urban planning was practiced earlier than 1500 BC, dealing in advance with issues such as population density, environmental issues, sanitation, and transportation. Over 2000 years ago, each continent, North America [Anasazi and Hopewell] and South America [Moche], as well as Mesoamerica [Olmec and Maya], had cultures that displayed evidence of comprehensive preplanning in their city models. These included concepts such as choosing city sites, laying out the entire area around city centres, piping in water through enclosed basalt aqueducts, building dams for water conservation, solid waste transportation and burial, angled streets to allow for public water collection cisterns, and angled roofs for personal water tanks.

By the 1300s and 1400s the area of Lake Texcoco, in modern day Mexico, had aqueducts sophisticated enough to supply year-round water to households for personal use. By building causeways over swamps and combining this with a transportation grid, the government could provide water, as well as waste removal, operated by a thriving local merchant class. The government hired over 1000 workers to keep the city clean, at a time when all European cities were using their streets as open sewers for waste. This deeply ingrained practice persisted for centuries in Europe and in the Americas under colonial rule. Boston was known to still be dealing with street sewage well into the 1800s when they had trouble introducing sanitation bylaws to fight disease.

The urban cleanliness cited above was coupled in this case with public health measures. Personal hygiene and clean water made the work of their hospitals easier. In Mesoamerica, Aztec public hospitals meant the poor could be cared for by specialist doctors, midwives, and nurses. The existence of prenatal care, early sex education, and mental health physicians shows the breadth of that example. It was the world's first publicly funded healthcare system.

Another example of Indian government innovation was the very specific labour laws protecting the workers and their families in the difficult Andean mining industries. Only men who were part of a married couple worked in mining. There existed a formal family division of labour, rules around seasonal conditions and rest periods, supplied provisions, and mandatory removal of sick miners. Miners were rotated on a schedule with

The government hired over 1000 workers to keep the city clean, at a time when all European cities were using their streets as open sewers for waste.

feasts and festivals playing a large role. The contrast is stark when compared to the Europeans, who operated mines from the 1500s onward, in some of the most notoriously brutal conditions in the history of labour.

Tax systems varied between voluntary setups in North America, and the more common tribute methods elsewhere, whereby workers contributed labour for the maintenance of roads, building of pyramids, maintenance of suspension bridges, civil engineering, farming, etc. In return, a social welfare system meant no one went hungry, including those injured by their work.

Disability rights laws also protected all blind and disabled citizens, providing them with special work provisions, encouragement to marry and participate in mainstream activities and having basic needs met when they could not entirely furnish a livelihood for themselves. The elderly and those with chronic diseases were also taken care of.

This setup was in stark contrast to Europe. Rulers normally ignored the disabled who were typically homeless and living on the streets. The Inquisition of the 1400s meant the killing of disabled throughout Europe. They were thought to be possessed by demons. England's debtor prison system came to include these same handicapped and poor individuals, a concept moved overseas with the implementation of "poor farms" and "county farms" in the United States.

The thousands of subcultures in the Western Hemisphere were destined to evolve into thousands of political systems and smaller subsystems. It is the sum total of these contributions that are worthy of note and worthy of study. The totality of the distilled ideas for government astounds Indigenous Studies students worldwide. Ideally, the recognition for these inspirational ideas will follow at some point. Until that happens, we can continue to be inspired by the innovative thoughts themselves, and concentrate on putting the better ones to use in humanity's upward trek.

≋ CHAPTER 4 ≋
Technology

Nothing catches our attention like technology, right? The world is quick to adopt a desirable change nowadays, and it was quick to adopt a desirable change then. Prior to 1492, any community through the ages would naturally have infrastructure with its divisions. The difference in the world after 1492 is the appearance of new ways of doing things within those infrastructures, the introduction of techniques and products from around the world, and the sharing or trading of all things desirable to others. Now I share information in an attempt to impress you, the reader, with exciting information you may or may not have on your radar.

Road System in the Andes

The road system in the Andes was very intriguing and engineers still study it today. It's a fascinating story and a wonderful accomplishment. Yet even though it is interesting, the basics are not generally known and not taught to any of our children in school. It's not taught to anybody at all. I don't know why.

The Andean road system was started around AD 800 to 1200 by the Wari, Tiwanaku, and Chimor cultures but it wasn't finished by the Inca until 600 or 700 years ago. Either of the two main roadways, if placed in Canada, would stretch from Newfoundland to Vancouver. If stretched across the U.S., each roadway would extend from New York to Los Angeles. The Incas inherited most of this infrastructure from previous civilizations, but used the road system to keep their empire as one. Of the two main highways, one was along the coast and one was in the mountains, and both were similar in length. The roads averaged anywhere from 9 to 15 feet across. A few places were as small as 5 feet across and other areas were as wide as 82 feet across.

There were many subsidiary roads and routes joining different areas, including the two main roads. At one point I had been teaching there were 40,000 kilometres (25,000 mi.) of roadway and I would say, "What does 40,000 kilometres sound like? That's the distance around the earth." It was an impressive number. Satellite technology allowed researchers to discover the total amount of roadway within the entire road system isn't 40,000 km, but 225,000 km (140,000 mi.) of routes plus highway. Needless to say, I've changed my teaching. This road system is still in use today.

It was the local people who built, created, and maintained the road system, and the work was treated as a tribute to the Empire. One of the reasons for this approach was the work, when completed by local people, would incorporate their knowledge of local materials, other roadways, and topography such as mountains.

In addition to their ability to build lasting roadways, the knowledge and skills of these mountain-based people allowed them to produce systems with very good irrigation, runoff, stabilizing, and terracing. These talents coincided with their ability to create great water systems. Most of these travel facilities are still in place today because of the thoroughness of their techniques. They routinely dug through mountains. They built causeways up to 13 km (8 mi.) long. They also had access to the use of gondolas and ferries when gorges were too wide to have a suspension bridge system.

The suspension bridge, another gift to the world from the Native Indians, was unknown in Europe at that time. Suspension bridges are bridges where the deck hangs from cables and there is nothing underneath the bridge deck. These types of bridges were built to cross large gorges. Europeans were scared to go on the suspension bridges, and they did not build or utilize them in Europe until the 1800s.

The Inca predecessors always built two suspension bridges next to the other; the largest ones were up to 200 feet long. The practice of building two suspension bridges next to each other existed so one bridge could be maintained and worked on while the second bridge was in use. They were all built with textiles and fibres so they needed a maintenance schedule. It's also probable the nobility traveled on one of the bridges, and the common folk journeyed across on the other bridge; but the people were in a position where the roads were open all the time.

They also designed cables similar to today's steel cables to support their suspension bridges. They would make rope of a certain size, and then braid three of those together into a larger size, then braid these pieces into larger sizes, etc. Some of these suspension bridges had 1-foot diameter cables supporting them.

Another feature of the Andean road system is the infrastructure that enhanced the network. For instance, they placed distance markers every 7 kilometres (4.3 mi.). All along the road they had small weigh stations where people could stay. The stations were stocked with food, and in some cases weapons, but mostly they were supplied with provisions travellers would need during their journeys. They also had smaller houses (booths) and about every 10 kilometres runners were stationed.

Some of these suspension bridges had 1-foot diameter cables supporting them.

Their road system helped them run their empire. The empire was organized so news would travel throughout the empire utilizing the runners. It was like a relay system. The runners would travel 10 kilometres (6 mi.) with the messages. Some of the messages were instructions and orders, and some of them contained news of what was going on in the empire. Using this relay system, they could cover 250 kilometres (155 mi.) a day, which meant they could cover 2000 kilometres (1250 mi.) in just over a week.

Another interesting point is the way they travelled with their messages. Their system of communication consisted of using multiple attached strings of different lengths and colours, along with different placement positions of knots on the strings. These beautifully crafted aids are called quipu. A few decades ago, artifact specialists began discovering this was not simply artwork. Now they realize it's a fairly sophisticated, mostly numerical language. The runners carried these types of messages so the information wasn't distorted along the way. They would travel the breadth of the empire with these messages. The quipu are still scattered in museums around the world even today known as Indigenous art.

This is how the road system in the Andes was developed.

The Indians in these areas displayed a great amount of knowledge to produce such a wonder of the world, and the Spanish were well aware of their superior skills in that area. Over time, the uniqueness of the accomplishment became less and less celebrated, until it finally reached a point of near invisibility.

Rubber

Indians gave rubber to the world. The Industrial Revolution is what today's civilization is really founded upon. Steel and rubber and petroleum are the three primary ingredients that made the Industrial Revolution possible. Rubber played a large part. Charles Goodyear is the "inventor" who patented rubber vulcanizing in 1844 after the non-vulcanized rubber-coated bags he sold the U.S. Post Office failed to hold up in the heat. In his search for a solution, he stumbled upon the same process the Olmec had used.

The truth is this process had been discovered 3000 years before. Ancient inventors needed to discover how to vulcanize rubber because raw rubber isn't useful for any length of time. The powder from morning glory plants furnished early rubber producers with the sulfur needed for the finished product. Olmec and other early Indigenous in the south waterproofed tarps, baskets, ropes, sandals, bottles, and capes. Later civilizations founded the rubber industry, which grew in massive proportions during the pre-Colonial American era and then exploded on the world scene in the 1500s.

They were not just playing games with rubber and inventing basketball and soccer-like pastimes. As mentioned, they had practical uses for rubber. They had waterproof ponchos and clothing. They had rubber boots and raincoats. Shoes worn by Indians were quickly adopted by many European settlers when they first arrived in the Americas. When travelling with natives, settlers tended to borrow the Indians' backup pair from their knapsacks because they considered the design and materials superior to the hard leather European boots.

This was not unusual. Many, many things were adopted by Europeans. Remember, they lived closely with the Indians for those first few generations. They lived beside each other. They travelled together. Their towns were sometimes merged. There were many assimilation examples which took place from one side to the other, back and forth. They were peers and co-equals. But, it's all been submerged in today's world and it has happened on purpose.

Ecological sustainability

The Indigenous had a sustainable ecology, up and down these two continents. Certainly, they were excellent stewards of the land. It doesn't mean they left the land unchanged, as in the pristine wilderness myths. On the contrary, it means they treated the entire continent as a sort of garden on a continental scale.

In South America, the terracing they first adopted was not found anywhere else in the world. Indians of the South American Andes Mountains invented terrace farming. They lived in the mountains, so flatlands were rare. In turn, they simply created flat land by building steps of land for agriculture down the mountainside. Terraced hillsides resemble stairsteps. It was this type of terracing they utilized with their mountain farming. When sweet potatoes and corn were introduced to China, terracing techniques were likewise introduced. The dynasty ordered tens of millions of peasants to begin planting these vegetables on their hills. These two crops are very easy to grow in the tough conditions of mountains, poor quality soil, and low rainfall.

It is now believed much of the fruit growing wild in South America is actually from ancient Indian orchards planted long ago. Early inhabitants of the Americas reshaped their continental landscape in all areas, including Mesoamerica. In North America, the best example is the burning of the woods.

Northern Indians burned the woods in a continuous cycle, spring or fall. Of course, this helped with the growth of the trees and with the undergrowth in the forests. It helped control bugs. It made hunting and travel easier because the trees were spaced out.

The burning behaviour is commented on by many of the settlers who came in the earliest periods to North America; so is the spacing of the trees. For thousands of years the landscape was controlled this way. Ironically, depopulated Indigenous nations meant the burning stopped, and the high percentage of cleared farmland filled in with reforested areas. So, the "dense wilderness" widely reported by early settlers was actually a recent phenomenon resulting from the disrupted civilizations no longer burning their surrounding forests.

Another example of ecological sustainability in North America is in the realm of animal husbandry. There are only 38 animals in the world that can be domesticated. Of course, in the other landmass, which is Eurasia and Africa, they had the cow, the oxen, the camel, and the horse. Native Indians didn't have the large domesticated animals in the Western Hemisphere. In North and South America, there were no animals capable of holding a human or capable of pulling heavy loads. The 300-pound llama could carry some goods and could also carry a child. But llamas and alpacas couldn't carry a full-sized person or deal with pulling loads or ploughs.

The Native Indians just did not have domesticated animals like other cultures. The camels and horses native to the Western Hemisphere were wiped out in the last Ice Age. Therefore, as the inhabitants evolved, they didn't have any of those types of options to draw upon.

However, there are examples of animal "husbandry," in a sense, when it came to food. Of course, they did eat meat. They did domesticate turkeys, and they hunted for meat. Some nations actually created plains, over a period of many, many generations to bring buffalo from the middle of the North American continent further east. They created plains the buffalo could roam. Since they were unable to domesticate animals for meat, they would sometimes gradually move the animals into their area. This meant they didn't have to go so far and wide on their hunting expeditions, while trying to carry enough food back to their home areas.

In these cases, visitors would see a pattern of visible consequences from the thousands of years of Indian occupation. Then after 1492, major changes occur for the Indigenous. Disruption becomes the order of the day. Colonization builds itself upon an existing framework of Indian effort and accomplishments. The Indigenous are artfully pushed aside over a period of dozens or hundreds of years. Then one day "poof" and Indians never existed, except as collections of pitiable mirages and clichés. Today, we have to fight just to show the world important things happened here long ago, too.

Lifestyle

At some point along this path I'm creating, I want you to look around you as you drive, as you eat, as you listen to peoples' words. Feel the contributions in our world today. They won't all be obvious because the world has added most of our changes recently. Search for the continuity to the past Indian endeavours. Stretch to see past the fog of supposed European roots to everything in your view. Remember it's untrue that everything emanated from "over there." Many inventions from the Indians impact our current lifestyle. Many were created by the Native Indians and used by the Europeans themselves.

Europeans adopted hammocks, written about in Columbus' first accounts. Cotton and agave hammocks were used in the West Indies, South America, and Mesoamerica. They became standard gear on sailing vessels around the world.

Steam rooms and sweat lodges in the Americas have been a

constant down through the millennia, even as other worldwide cultures variably took up and abandoned the practice.

The oldest Olmec hematite mirrors, from 1500 BC, used a grinding and polishing technology which remains a mystery today. Underarm deodorants, sunscreens, and insect repellants for crops or living quarters all varied greatly from area to area according to what natural products were available.

Among the first sports helmets in history, the 3000-year-old Olmec basketball helmet resembles the early twentieth century leather football helmets. While the Olmec peoples played a game very similar to basketball, the helmet was worn along with protective padding such as gloves, knee pads, hip pads, and footwear. Since they had invented and perfected latex rubber balls, they are considered the early inventors of two types of basketball, soccer, and football even though we think of these games as recent creations.

Stickball was played all over North America throughout history. These Northern Indian games are the only ones from the world's ancient times able to be linked to modern ice hockey and field hockey, as they are played today.

Colonists on the frontier adopted most of the Indigenous clothing; breeches, footwear, moccasins, leggings, and fringed clothing. Trousers, thought by fashion historians to have been introduced by way of China, have been used in North America for an incredible 25,000 years. Originally, Inuit tailored garments consisted of two leggings sewn together with seams running up the front and the rear. Both Arctic and Subarctic cultures are known to have produced these articles of clothing. In post-colonial times, impractical European hose, pantaloons, and knickers gave way over time, until upper-class colonists and Europeans adopted trousers in earnest around the time of the French Revolution.

As is seen repeatedly, the settlers of regions far and wide copied the Indigenous habits in diverse ways like trousers, sports, and clothing. Eventually, Europeans came to believe they themselves had made up many of these contributions and gifts to the world we take for granted today.

Building

As seen so often when mankind advances, some aspects of different world civilizations show them being behind the average and some aspects might be ahead of the average. But all of the peoples of the world went at the same overall pace. The beliefs about parts of the world being backwards while others were way ahead is proving to be unfounded. People love to create structures, and Indians found their own novel developments.

Concrete was invented independently and used after 300 BC. Home insulation appeared in the form of double walls, wall airspaces, outside windbreaks, draft-blocking entranceway designs, and semi-underground styles.

Western tribes in North America were using asphalt 10,000 years ago and trading it so extensively they created a culture centered on its use as caulking and as a sealant for canoes and baskets.

As mentioned earlier, aqueducts were used to bring water into large cities in Mesoamerica. The use of gravity in aqueducts dates back to 1500 BC with many of the valleys in Mesoamerica and South America containing water engineering projects. One Chicama Valley aqueduct, dating from around 100 BC, is nearly 50 feet in the air and 1.6 kilometres (1 mi.) long.

Western Hemisphere plumbing projects also pre-dated Roman water systems by 1500 years and were again developed independently of the Middle East and Mediterranean cultures. Building upon Olmec innovations, the later Aztec of AD 1200 had personal restrooms in many residences along with public restrooms. They implemented a system with dual fresh water, plaster-lined canals which allowed clean water to be piped in while the second conduit was cleaned or repaired. Urine was transported out of the communities by similarly designed plumbing systems.

Copper tubing was used in Peruvian areas around AD 1100 for plumbing. But the first metalworkers in the world were the early Paleo-Indians of the Great Lakes who used copper tubing for pan pipes and creating tubular beads. Maya also developed copper tubing around 1500 BC. The technology was used to produce hollow drill bits for working stone and to prepare teeth for fillings and inlays.

Stonemasonry skills are evident in all parts of the Western Hemisphere covering all cultures and all time periods. The pyramids are not only the largest and tallest in the world they are by far the most abundant. The Olmec, although they are the oldest of dozens of stonemason cultures, are considered the greatest stone sculptors in the pre-contact Americas. They are best known for their 20-ton stone carvings.

Spanish reporters famously wrote about the precision of the cutting of blocks in the Inca homelands. With their "cellular stonework" technology, they carved irregular polygon blocks that fit together into walls so precise a razor blade could not be inserted between the fitted multi-ton rocks several hundred years later; a period covering many earthquakes which

...Aztec of AD 1200 had personal restrooms in many residences along with public restrooms.

destroyed neighbouring areas in some cases.

Some of the precision exacting construction sites also involved 1,800 men carrying 100-metric-ton stones 35 kilometres (22 mi.). Ollantaytambo's largest stone is 140,000 kilograms (308,000 lbs.). Early White-dominated archaeologist groups could not believe the precision of the Peruvian projects and the Mississippian Culture mounds, prompting them to promote mistaken theories suggesting a mysterious archaic culture must have created the massive structures.

You probably have acquaintances who have visited famous World Heritage Sites in parts of our landmass here between the Atlantic and the Pacific. They marvel at the amazing things they are seeing, and then return home to the Eurocentric assumptions all of this was all completed by some remote past peoples and had nothing to do with today or the colonial period of 1492 to present. When they think like that they are being duped by the conditioning of our faulty worldviews. Civilizations *were* flourishing here in 1492. The people had not all disappeared or become backward prior to Europeans arriving here. Unfortunately, those are all lies.

Energy Forms

The most amazing of all pre-contact inventions was the production of electricity through the use of chemicals. It was the Moche, arising around 200 BC, who utilized copper as both an anode and cathode to produce electric current used for electroplating.

During the procedure they perfected the complex art of plating with gold and silver. The invention required the development of a corrosive liquid to dissolve the gold, a strong acid with a pH of 9. The amount of knowledge required to accomplish this *cannot* be overemphasized. Sir Humphrey Davies is credited with electrolysis of fused salts in the early 1800s, but the Moche, in fact, preceded Europeans by well over a thousand years.

Considered by Europeans as savages, Indigenous peoples managed this monumental achievement hundreds of years before. The intelligence needed for this accomplishment spanned scientific understanding, electricity fundamentals, chemistry, organized experiments and data, and reproduced laboratory results until an actual electroplating industry was created.

Like countless occasions in our cockeyed Western history versions, a similar situation occurred with petroleum. Edwin Drake is credited as the first to discover oil in America and dig for it. But he was *not* the first. Four hundred years earlier, American Indians in the exact same area, today's Pennsylvania, drilled pits into the ground to collect seeping oil.

Evidence of a widespread and sophisticated oil-collection effort suggests a much earlier discovery since support timbers in 20-foot oil pits reveal carbon dating to year 1430. Thus, the practice had likely been developing for a long time. A large number of drill sites were found in organized arrangements. However, once again, unable to admit the Indian tribes were capable of such advanced technology, J.A. Caldwell and others reported the pits were the work of a race of people who occupied the territory prior to the Indians.

Solar fire starters were Olmec devices similar to the polished mirrors still baffling researchers today. The concave polished surface of various iron-ore-containing materials produced the ability to concentrate a reflection and produce hot rays capable of starting a fire. The 3,500-year-old devices still operate today.

How did we arrive here, a place where kids grow up learning about somewhere else's history? Greece, Rome, Mesopotamia, Egypt, Saxony, Mongolia and on and on; anywhere but here will do. How did we make our own land mass non-existent? This is *our* home, isn't it? Its people have been made invisible in such a slow, methodical way even well-meaning scientific specialists add to the symphony of lies without even realizing what they're doing.

Metals

A fair amount of colonial history comes down to metallurgy. It was the seeking of precious metals that motivated the exploration from Europeans. The highly developed skills of the Indigenous had produced thousands of years' worth of high-quality, high-quantity gold and silver items. The brutality and audacity of the conquering savages from Europe placed them in a position to succeed. Their greed knew no bounds. Roomful after roomful of intricate precious valuables were melted down and ended up in European treasuries. There is little doubt the balance of power in the modern world can be traced back to the successful theft of these precious metals.

South American techniques passed from the Chavin metal foils of 1400 BC to the highly skilled Moche of 200 BC. Moche mined, smelted, electroplated gold and silver, annealed, soldered, and alloyed all combinations of metals and precious metals. They produced astonishingly intricate jewelry, tweezers, bells, and scalpels. Their gold-plating techniques included using acids alone, adhering thin gold foil sheets, and electroplating. Moche traditions were carried on by the Inca, who later perfected their own elaborate multi-step procedure for plating gold in such a way that Andean gold work is recognizable and contains a unique shiny surface after the final burnishing.

In Mesoamerica, the Aztec were preceded by the Mixtec and also taught by the Toltec. Their quantities of gold overwhelmed the Spanish. Still, the newcomers were overwhelmed by the sophistication of the techniques and the quality and detail of the gold and silver pieces, compared to Europe. Even their other uses for metal were impressive. Mayan dental drill bits were hollow styles of all sizes and varieties, including larger ones for working with stone. They left donut-shaped circular holes. Drilling was done in stages, so the protruding cylinder could be broken off for the next round of drilling.

Baffin Inuit produced blades of iron, also found in tools in northern Pacific areas. But Indians rarely worked with iron, even though the Great Lakes areas were well known 6,000 to 7,000 years ago for widely traded copper fish hooks, knives, pendants, picks, axes, wedges, and drill bits which look like today's drills. They are considered the earth's earliest at annealing and forming metals in this way.

Smelting operations typically used small ovens with blow tubes to work tin, bronze, silver, gold, copper, and arsenic. Metallurgists believe the scarcity of iron ore deposits meant those types of iron smelting skills never became widespread enough to gain popularity even though Egyptians were producing small iron products 5000 years ago.

Platinum, being the hardest and rarest metal in the world, was impossible to melt with any known standard furnace technique. Yet platinum *was* being worked in pre-contact Ecuador where the sintering of metals was first invented. That difficult process blended platinum and gold to lower the melting point enough to produce platinum art and jewelry. Platinum work was unknown in Europe until the nineteenth century.

Casting of copper pieces led to the invention of lost-wax gold casting around AD 100. The tool or ornament piece was first made of wax or plaster core covered in wax. The wax model was then covered with thick clay to create the mold. Heating then melted the wax leaving the cast ready to accept molten metal. Mesoamerican gold makers would eventually live in their own neighbourhoods and create formal guild organizations.

Even though much of their work was stolen and melted down and shipped to Europe, we have enough remaining Indian pieces to sort through the traditions of metal work that so dazzled the Europeans. Those traditions began 2,000 years before ships ever visited the hemisphere. The rich history of metal work has been forgotten and hidden as skilled craftspeople were forced to adapt to the odd techniques of the conquerors.

The Many Developments

The wide spectrum of Indian technology contributions reminds us of our wide variety of technologies today. Most of our everyday systems trace back, in some way, to this land's original inhabitants. Look at the components making up the complex world all around us. Trace each one back hundreds and hundreds of years to feel a fresh truism; all the peoples of the world made our life what it is today.

Plant classifications varied by area. Non-Indian scientists only recently began seriously studying some of the sophisticated and workable complete systems. For example, Aztec horticulturists divided plants by Form, General Use, and Economic Use with each having three main classifications. Plants listed under Form were divided up into trees, bushes, or herbs. Those listed under General Use were divided into food, medicinal, or ornamental, and Economic Use listings were separated into clothing, building, or other.

In Europe, botanist Carolus Linneaus' eighteenth century classifications used stamens and pistols, looking at their numbers and attachment. However, the ethnocentrically dismissed Aztec system above predates the European arrangement for plant naming by 400 years, and other complete naming systems existed as well.

The absence of the wheel and axle is always mentioned, along with steel, as the look-no-further sign of inferiority when it came to Indians. But wheels and axles were found on children's pull-toy animals. This invention, as early as 1000 BC, took place in spite of the fact draft animals were not present. Round spindle wheels were also used to spin yarn from fibre. Since anthropologists claimed the wheel was the true test of whether a society was a civilization, the discovery of the toys in 1880 was largely ignored. To acknowledge them would have been to admit the Indians did, in fact, have a civilization. When many more were found in the twentieth century, scientists were forced to take it more seriously. The question of whether the Indians in fact "had a civilization" was revisited many times during the 1900s, until the question itself grew to become a quaint anachronism within the slowly progressing scientific community.

The Yucatan's Olmec civilization had working compasses a thousand years before they were independently invented in China and then Western Europe.

Vertical and horizontal looms for weaving were definitely used everywhere in the Americas beginning from about 2000 BC, a date which corresponds to the time all great civilizations were advancing their weaving skills. Andean textiles are 5,000 to 7,000 years old which is equivalent to the oldest known use of these practices. But, the Rio Guayas' area may have worn woven clothing 6,000 to 9,000 years ago. These determinations rely on interpreting murals and statues since woven materials disintegrate over time. Those time frames would represent a much earlier use of weaving than the oldest Indus Valley (India) model. Whether or not the Western Hemisphere was more advanced or accomplishing the feat around the same time is not really relevant. However, look no further for the reinforcement and entrenchment of our faulty worldviews. Typical histories of all types do not have OUR land mass in their viewing lens at all.

Consider this, most histories of weaving and looms follow a very familiar pattern: First, a review of Egypt circa BC then some Bible references, and then it moves into AD. "By 700 AD, horizontal and vertical looms could be found in Asia, Africa, and Europe." History then moves onto medieval Europe, Colonial America, and the Industrial Revolution. Nothing is mentioned from the Americas whatsoever. No reference is made to the Andean large-cloth vertical looms in 1000 BC, or their tapestry weaving by 400 BC. No mention is made of the early gauzes, stripes, checks, twills, brocades, double cloth, or open-work. No one references the popularity in stores around the world today of Guatemalan garments crafted by weavers on the same back-strap looms their ancestors used thousands of years ago.

Paper usage again brings up the issue of European and Western thinking, along with its smugness and arrogance. Asian and European papers, made of pulp and dating from 100 BC in China, are characterized as "true" paper. In yet another untold story, Mesoamerican paper of high quality was being produced around 1000 BC and used to produce books by AD 700.

The inner bark of the wild fig tree was utilized for most of the paper technologies. By AD 1200, paper was in demand and communities devoted to paper production sprung up around larger fig orchards. Most towns had their own unique processes, including sheets and rolls and codices and binding systems. In the 1500s, Europeans documented their methods of production, which are considered the same methods used by their ancestors 1200 to 1500 years earlier. They also wrote the paper was thicker and whiter than the paper in Europe at the time.

In the 1560s, all books became illegal and thousands of books were ordered burned by the Spanish monarchy. Spain ruled the entire area and they were using the common vanquisher techniques, which meant outlawing local language, traditions, religious practices, culture, and independent trade capacity. Paper was targeted for destruction rather than exploitation because the monarchy did whatever the church instructed them to do. The church had surmised Christianity would not flourish while the Indigenous enjoyed the use of their books in a language indecipherable to the Spanish. Thus, the paper industry ended in Mesoamerica, although one style of this "*amate*" paper is still used in parts of Mexico today.

Adding up the developments, we see many of them are great accomplishments! However, it's traditionally an invisible hemi-

Adding up the developments, we see many of them are great accomplishments! However, it's traditionally an invisible hemisphere to the world's historians.

sphere to the world's historians. It isn't difficult to find these words when looking for ancient historical info. "By such-and-such date, the _____ [fill in your choice of innovation] could be found in Asia, Africa and Europe."

Europeans visited and quickly took over areas such as the West Indies, South America and Mesoamerica. North America was taken over in a slower process, but with similar results. Whether we examine Spain and Portugal to the south, or England, France, and Netherlands to the north, Indians were originally known to be peers and co-equals. Even during the more brutal takeovers of the Spanish, the same premise applies. They knew they were facing a formidable people, on a par with themselves. The Europeans could be unfriendly or friendly in their methods, but the monarchies in Europe tried to strategize their takeovers carefully.

But history forgot. People forgot. It didn't happen overnight, but it happened everywhere. Indians first started disappearing from the real landscape. Then they started disappearing from our mental landscapes. Undoing the legacy of ignorance isn't going to be easy. It starts with a few simple light bulbs going on in dominant-culture minds.

≋ CHAPTER 5 ≋
Food

Seventy-five percent of the foods grown in the world today are known to be gifts of the Native Indian, even though our land mass comprises only 30% of the planet. What a great and little-known contribution!

Since the dawn of civilization, obtaining enough to eat has been the biggest difficulty we as humans have faced. In the Americas they've been busy for many thousands of years finding some of our solutions. It isn't generally known or admitted that their impact was so pronounced in the area of food production.

Famines were a common scourge put up with by Europeans during the centuries leading up to 1492, especially in the northern regions, including Russia. South America gave the world the potato and Mesoamerica gave the world corn and both had immediate impact. The potato saved the Irish and most of northern Europe during many of their massive famines, and corn saved southern Europe. The yield from wheat was only a fraction of the yield per acre from corn, and European farmers were amazed to see the quantities of food produced on Indian farms. The people of the Western Hemisphere put

Europeans on the map, and one of the ways was by helping Europeans solve their famine difficulties.

When harvested and stored, wheat, barley, and rye were vulnerable to marauding armies and overbearing landlords. These pilferers had difficulty when farmers were introduced to another gift of the Indian – potatoes. Potatoes could be left underground until people were ready to harvest them.

Corn and sweet potato, gifts of the American Indian, grew easily compared to rice and wheat and gave much larger yields. Low-grade soil, low-moisture areas, hills and grades, and high altitude all gave way to these two staple vegetables. As a result, they were being grown in many parts of the world and on every continent by 1550. The world was ready for some agricultural breakthroughs to help support their populations.

The Inca in South America, building on previous civilizations, gave 80 food plants to the world. Now, if that isn't a magnificent contribution to today's civilization, you have to wonder what is. They gave more food plants to the world than all of Europe combined. The Czechs, the English, the French, the Hungarians, the Greeks, the Scandinavians, the Germans, the Spanish, the Romanians, the Russians, the Swiss, the Poles, the Italians, the Portuguese, and the rest of Europe, all combined together, did not give as many food plants as one Indian nation, the Inca from South America.

Many of us know about the three sisters made up of corn and beans and squash. In this trio, the corn provides the climbing structure for the beans, the beans provide nitrogen to the soil, and the squash leaves retain moisture and block sunlight to minimize weeds and bugs. Again, this practice took place all up and down the Americas and had been developed over thousands and thousands of years. There's a nutritional makeup to a three sisters' meal which provides a comprehensive diet. If you add an avocado, it is a 100% complete diet. Between them they contain all eight essential amino acids, a complex carbohydrate, and the essential fatty acids.

Beans contain protein. Every bean in the world, except for two, was a gift from the American Indian. The soybean and horse bean came from China. The chickpea is sometimes counted as well, and it originated in the Middle East. All other beans came from the Western Hemisphere. Because beans are a great source of protein, they become important when a culture doesn't have enough meat or fish. Another example of plant protein is nuts, where Indians have contributed 60% of our nut species.

There were 300 different types of corn plants, including the "hybrid" corn the White man claims to have discovered in the middle of the twentieth century. Some of you may remember growing up with "Indian corn," a kind of goofy corn nobody ate. It was only used for decoration. The use of Indian corn served to diminish the image and role the Indian had on corn; the one gift they are universally given worldwide credit for "gifting." Many people will say Indians gave corn to the world, but then that's where any recognition of contributing to world civilization ends. Perhaps you recall seeing rectangular "corn cribs" along the sides of highways? Those corn storage facilities were still being used in the twentieth century, adopted from Indians and virtually unchanged from ancient times.

Over a period of countless generations, food such as corn, potato, sweet potato [unrelated], tomato, pepper, squash, beans, and quinoa was bred and developed on Indian farms by Indian farmers, and it was not growing out in the wild by any means. The tomato and peppers were all members of the nightshade family. The nightshade plant, a deadly poison, grew in Europe; hence the Spanish cut off the hands of natives who offered it to them thinking they were trying to poison them. The Europeans weren't able to turn the nightshade plants into a beautiful food to eat the way the Indians did. All the Indian foods showed greater change from their natural wild sister plants than the food plants of Asia or Africa or Europe. The Indians happen to have a natural gift for farming.

It is believed dozens of sprawling terrace facilities in the Andes are agricultural research centers used to grow thousands of plant variations and conduct hundreds of experiments lasting for generations. We know the food plants were bred in sophisticated ways. The amazing Machu Picchu of the Andes is considered by many to be one of these centers of food development and spiritual adulation.

The potato has been referred to as a world changer. Take a guess at how many potatoes there were. The Native Indians had 6,000 different types of potatoes in the Andes in South America, and still do today. Scientists are still not certain how many species are represented. It happened that very few types were transported around the world, but they have plenty more.

The Irish Potato is one of many names of items with misleading labels attached to them. Because the potato "saved Ireland" or "saved the world," it has a reputation as a food that actually altered history. But notice the name; it's called the Irish Potato. That's very misleading. It's symptomatic of the historical paradigms that have existed for 500 years and continue to exist today. We can make the Western Hemisphere Indigenous people invisible whenever we want.

In the next example, cotton, Europeans were so impressed by the fineness of the cotton cloth it was first mistaken for silk. They were experiencing South Sea cotton, still the finest cotton in the world today, and playing a large part in trade between the years 1000 and 1800. But there's that misleading name attached in our economies, Egyptian cotton. Clothes are labelled this way even though Egypt's crude short-haired cotton plants are not even grown commercially today. All of our cotton is South Sea cotton.

Besides Egyptian cotton and the Irish Potato, there's the Madagascar bean, Italian tomato, Rangoon bean, Jerusalem

The Irish Potato is one of many names of items with misleading labels attached to them.

artichoke, Idaho potato, French vanilla, Italian bean, Hawaiian pineapple, India rubber, Boston baked beans, french fries, Turkish tobacco, French bean, the turkey itself, Parisienne potatoes, Burma bean, Belgian chocolate, English walnuts, and the Turkish bath. The popularization of these foreign names is equal and opposite to the diminishing of the Indigenous in our Western culture.

We take credit in subtle ways that end up in our lexicons and in our collective psyche. Many ideas are just "out there" floating around, part of our unofficial guidebook. They are not easy to undo, because the lies are not only in textbooks. For generations, faulty worldviews and untruths have been woven into the fabric of playground talk, parents' comments, literature, jokes, grandparents' comments, church teachings, TV commercials, movies and TV shows. This is the unsanctioned "real" education we receive growing up, the type of learning having a greater impact in shaping our world than the public education system.

Globalization
From 1500 onward the world was looking at a globalization very similar to today's globalization. While today's era could

be called Globalization 2.0, the first globalization related to ships transporting goods and the connection of over 30 main ports around the world.

Globalization 1.0 started quickly. For example, Europe was already growing potatoes in the 1500s. Like the potato, there were many plants going abroad. Plus, it wasn't just food travelling across the world. You had ideas and thoughts travelling around the world. You had a lot of viruses and bacteria and microbes. You had clothing and art. You had slaves and indentured servants. You also had a lot of fish and animals and insects and worms and even smaller creatures. This transfer of goods and ideas is referred to as the Columbian Exchange.

This was not just beneficial fruits and vegetables being given as gifts and transforming societies. There were also undesirable species going into strange ecological systems. In a similar way to what happens today, an introduced species can seriously disrupt the balance of an ecological system. There were unintended consequences with wild animals and birds and plants. So a lot of cultures were changing dramatically due to things travelling, diseases not least among them in terms of having a huge impact.

Sweet potato and corn were mentioned as being world changers, and the best example is in China. The Chinese had mostly dynasties and were not much different from today when they wanted to make a change. They could change quickly. They would bring in an edict and the whole country would start doing it. The Chinese government instructed all their peasants to start growing sweet potatoes and corn, particularly in the hilly areas, because corn is very forgiving in terms of rainfall, where it grows, temperature, types of soil, even growing on mountains. Additionally, sweet potato and corn both have remarkable yields.

All down through world history, when populations grew, it was because they began to be properly fed. China's population doubled in the 200-year period when corn and sweet potatoes were given to them and they were instructed on how to grow them on terraced hills. Corn and sweet potato and potato are three examples among many world changers given to us by the Western Hemisphere natives, but downplayed by history.

More Agriculture Contributions

Domesticated and cultivated potatoes are known to date to 8000 BC and corn 7000 to 8000 BC, but the Ancient History Encyclopedia Agriculture Timeline doesn't seem to be aware of it [https://www.ancient.eu / timeline / Agriculture]. They list potatoes at 3000 BC and corn at 2700 BC.

Even though we are now in the twenty-first century, it seems it just wouldn't do for the Fertile Crescent to have competition from primitives. The Fertile Crescent is a crescent-shaped region where agriculture and early human civilizations like the Sumer and Ancient Egypt flourished due to inundations from the surrounding Nile, Euphrates, and Tigris rivers. In the competitive world of thought, the "primitive" land called the Americas must take their position a few rungs down on the ladder from the "other land mass" with their more sophisticated image.

Terraced farming techniques existed in many areas, in different forms, allowing hillside land cultivation and greatly increasing the maximum crop yields. Many ingenious irrigation systems allowed for slow controlled water of the stair-step style farming hills. A number of unchanged pre-contact farms are still in use today.

Fertilizers, in use since 3000 BC, reached a peak at a time when the Guano Islands had 100-foot-thick deposits of bird droppings. The islands were divided by the Incas so farmers in all of the districts could be assigned sections with the valuable fertilizer. By the 1700s, the Spanish were shipping the guano around the world, and in one 20-year period during the 1800s 11 million tons of guano was exported by Peru. This nitrogen-rich product is credited with beginning the modern era of agriculture in Europe.

Quinoa has been an important part of life in Andean culture for 5,000 years. It's a remarkable plant with multiple uses and nutritional properties well known to those societies. Quinoa seeds have twice the protein as corn, barley, or rice in a form more easily used by the body. They are high in the amino acid lysine, and relatively high in fat. Quinoa is a complete protein and contains calcium, iron, vitamin E, phosphorous, and B vitamins. Its carbohydrates are easier to digest than rye, millet, wheat, corn, or sorghum.

Quinoa was introduced into the North American market for the first time in 1984 in health food stores and has grown steadily in popularity. It is available nowadays in supermarkets. Other very popular basic southern staples not yet discovered in a wider sense are chia, amaranth, and manioc or cassava. Each has noteworthy and unique properties. There are also half a dozen other ancient, long-time staple food plants not even named in English yet.

American-bred turkeys were an immediate hit in Europe when introduced in 1498 and became a popular dish in England by the mid-1500s.

Quinoa has been an important part of life in Andean culture for 5,000 years.

Jerky is a popular food contribution and a Quecha word (Inca language). In today's market, this pre-contact meat-dehydrating technique is used with 20 different creatures. From their history lessons, many northerners have heard of "pemmican," which is just another form of jerky.

Instant foods such as potato flakes, parched beans, ground toasted cornmeal, and dried tortillas were available for use when travelling, well before their reinvention in the twentieth century.

Thousands of years ago, Andean civilizations also discovered the process of freeze-drying foods and still enjoy the freeze-dried potatoes today. The principle of freeze drying was largely ignored until the 1960s but today over 450 foods are freeze dried.

Ice fishing in the North and Northeast was part of Indian tradition. Typically, it was practiced with spears inside shelters which hid the fisherman from view from the fish. The harpoons used in Northern areas, from Alaska to Greenland, were the only ones in the world with sophisticated detachable points.

Since corn and Thanksgiving seem to be the only universally recognized Indian contributions, some notes about Thanksgiving are in order. The Wampanoag had six Thanksgiving festivals throughout the year. The first harvest commemorated in colonial societies had its roots in a meeting of 50 Puritans and 90 Indians under Chief Massasoit, where they consumed five deer brought by the Wampanoag, along with corn and wild turkey. A few other foods were included on the menu.

In the ensuing decades, war developed between the parties over land theft and conflicting values. After the Puritans won the war, Massasoit's son Metacom was killed, and Wampanoag and Algonquin bands were tracked down. All these Indians were either killed or escaped to the north, while the remainder were sold into slavery in the West Indies and the Mediterranean.

The tragic story for one group becomes the celebration story for the other. Could there be a more poignant example of Indians and European settlers being peers and co-equals with people then forgetting? Remember the repeating pattern in North America? The White visitors were permitted to become guests. The guests became intruders. The intruders became too numerous to deal with, and when strong enough they pushed their hosts out and took everything for themselves. Next, they gradually forgot what they did. After a long, drawn-out incremental shifting of thought, the peers and co-equals are thought by today's settlers to have disappeared. What a pity.

≋ CHAPTER 6 ≋
Health

Let's talk about some tangible gifts the Native Indians gave us to improve our health. These 3,500 Indigenous peoples certainly made great contributions to the better side of our world civilization. It wasn't too long ago we called it the "White man's civilization." People are a bit more aware today. All the peoples of the world have contributed equally to our modern civilization, and the Native Indian certainly gave a lot to the good side of that. It can easily be argued the Indian was more advanced and put the White man on the map.

Cleanliness was an important practice the Indians taught Europeans. Other significant gifts the Native Indians taught the settlers were nutrition and eating a proper diet, a sense of well-being, and the importance of being outside in the fresh air, exercising, and the use of medicines.

The influence of Western Hemisphere health practices has spread far and wide. Medicines were well developed throughout the Western Hemisphere. Depending on the area, hospitals and universal healthcare could be found. Mayans were performing brain surgery. Although they were later burned, some very sophisticated medical journals existed in the form of codices. The accordion-shaped codex was the most common form among hundreds of books they had. Hospitals were known to practice a form of nursing education wherein the nurses were placed into a hierarchical training system.

The early explorer Jacques Cartier recorded an episode of the many very well-illustrated dynamics at work on these two new continents. We now know the incident involves scurvy. On the St. Lawrence River in 1536, ice-bound in his ship near today's Montreal, he and his men were dying. Of the 110 men onboard, 25 had died and only ten were well enough to assist the other 75. A Huron chief showed Cartier how to prepare a tea from the ground bark of an evergreen and he instructed them to drink it every two days. Within eight days they were all cured.

The French were so impressed with the knowledge of this cure they dug up saplings of those trees with the purpose of introducing the cure in Europe. The saplings were later planted in the king's garden in France but were forgotten over time.

It's worth noting how Cartier repaid the natives for their life-saving hospitality. In classic European style, the healthy crew tricked and kidnapped the chief, four children, the chief's two sons, and three other adults. Cartier shipped them all over to Europe and all ten of the Huron people were dead soon after landing.

Sailors continued dying of scurvy for centuries afterward. Scurvy had afflicted Europeans for eons, and Vitamin C, or ascorbic acid, was the cure. Indians everywhere knew that. We know today history shows the cure was repeatedly discovered and forgotten and rediscovered. Egyptians were aware of it from 1500 BC. Hippocrates himself documented it. Yet, if you ask Siri or Google who discovered the cure for scurvy, you'll hear no hesitation. You'll be told it was James Lind, a Scottish physician, in 1747.

The Indians alone were responsible for launching the world-wide pharmacological industry that has led us to our brave new world of treatments and health aids. They had an under-standing of disease coming from outside the body, and they displayed knowledge of isolation from disease. All Indians re-lated food and living conditions to health and disease. In the 400 years the White man has dominated these two continents, there isn't one medicinal plant they've discovered not already known to the Indians. The cures for dysentery, malaria, scurvy, non-venereal syphilis, goiter, and other ailments all came from the Americas.

Aspirin, iodine, cocaine, save the baby, and many other med-icines were contributed. Antibiotics were used to treat wounds in Aztec, West Coast, and Eastern Woodland Indian cultures. Antiviral treatments were used to treat viral disease in North American Great Plains cultures. Today's forms of quinine, kaolin, ipecac, and guaiacum are virtually unchanged from pre-contact days. The Panama Canal, instrumental in winning the Second World War, may not have been built without qui-nine to treat malaria.

Our modern view of medicine, our mental image, if you will, too often pictures European apothecaries with chemists in lab coats, creating white powders or filling up glass beakers with solutions leading the way directly to today's brilliant array of

The Indians alone were responsible for launching the world-wide pharmacological industry that has led us to our brave new world of treatments and health aids.

magical pharmaceuticals, but medicine is another example of equal contributions from around the world. China and Europe had hospitals. Africa provided medicinal relief down through the ages. The Mideast provided doctors to almost all of the royal courts of Europe.

However, the kings and queens in Europe were not receiving very helpful healthcare. Until the late 1700s, illness was still considered a divine punishment for sins, which meant the sick in Europe commonly went untreated. Bloodletting was the all-purpose treatment, strenuously argued for by European medical experts well into the 1800s. Moreover, the upper class and lower class did not differ much in the treatments they received. The lower classes in Europe in 1492 had no doctors or hospitals, had limited herbs supplied from a pharmacist, or hoped for the best from their barbers, who performed necessary surgery because they had sharp tools.

To put it simply, Indigenous health was much better than that of Europeans. Remember, they tried very hard to teach Europeans. Like other areas of endeavour, multiple ironies can be spotted when we view events through our modern lens. The Indigenous of the Western Hemisphere helped the world become healthier, and helped Europe recover from the lost centuries of the Dark Ages. The Europeans originally transported only information that fit comfortably into their own knowledge structures. Better techniques were shared or urged by the natives, but were typically adopted by Europeans much later. By the time adopted practices became widespread and useful to the West, they had moved on to their superiority mindset, giving Indians little or no credit for our foundations of healthy living.

Medical Tools and Techniques

We know the European written reports going back to Europe had a lot of impact on history, and nowhere is it more evident than in the medical field. Although much was lost in the scramble for gold and conquest, the infusion of information from Spaniards about American Indian surgery and medicine did much to fuel the growing scientific curiosity that marked the Renaissance period.

Many useful tools were first utilized by Native Indians. Prior to European contact, forceps were a well-established tool, particularly for head trauma operations. Andean and Mesoamerican cultures used obsidian and other materials for surgical scalpels, before 1000 BC. Later pre-contact cultures had metal scalpel technology, particularly silver scalpels shaped like lobster tails. But obsidian remained the preferred tool, because the edge, when flint knapped or chipped, is superior to metal scalpels.

Metal scalpels, even today, tear the cells, whereas obsidian moves between them due to its extreme sharpness. Incisions from obsidian flint blades stop bleeding almost immediately and begin healing. Only laser technology from the late twentieth century matches obsidian in this regard.

Prior to meeting Europeans, needles from thin animal bones were shaped and bevelled into an object similar to today's hypodermic needles. With these tools, the medical people could irrigate wounds, inject medication, or remove fluids. Even still, Alexander Wood is credited by many medical historians as inventing the syringe much later in 1853.

In North America, small animal bladders were added to create the bulb syringe. In Mesoamerica and South America, rubber served the same purpose as the bladder and invention of the rubber-bulb style of syringe is normally credited to Mesoamerican culture. The Northern Seneca had also devised a detachable nipple pouch for small babies, which was used in a similar way disposable nursing bottles are used today.

Hippocrates from 400 BC is hailed and revered as the "world's first physician." But, of course, there were doctors all over the world. A South American Paracas doctor's bag from

1300 BC contained cloths, obsidian scalpels, suturing needles and thread, spatulas, cotton balls, and bandages. Doctors' bags showed a great similarity across all North American culture groups at the time of Columbus. Some of the supplies you would see include pharmaceuticals, scalpels, lancets, mortars, pestles, bandages, tube drains, etc.

Medical practice had evolved into a set of specialised endeavours among the pre-contact Aztecs. General practitioners were accompanied by specific branches: eye doctors, dentists, ear doctors, interns, pharmacists, obstetricians, and surgeons.

By 1492, surgeons were important specialists everywhere throughout the Americas. The origins are traced to the Olmec of 3,000 to 3,500 years ago. As long as 3,000 years ago, South American surgeons began practicing brain surgery with results reported by medical anthropologists studying human remains. Their 85% survival rate compares favourably to the 50% survival rate in Western medicine brain surgery at the turn of the twentieth century.

Other practices found through the Americas included surgical drainage, unsurpassed bone traction or countertraction techniques, standardized cataract removal, skin grafts, effective anesthetics, and asepsis (sterile field) operating conditions, a noteworthy accomplishment on its own.

So many great accomplishments have been erased it has became necessary for history to forget the civilized attributes of these supplanted peoples.

Wellness

Because of their well-known history of written codices, and due to European reporting, it's well-known Mesoamerican doctors engaged in detailed medical research using scientific methods. The medicinal use for over 1200 plants was recorded and kept updated and improved through a series of ongoing experiments. Prescription amounts were well known.

Their 85% survival rate compares favourably to the 50% survival rate in Western medicine brain surgery at the turn of the twentieth century.

But not all cultures used books and written methods, as in the Mesoamerican example. Many Western Hemisphere cultures relied on oral tradition to pass information from healer to healer. The practices were just as thorough and sophisticated, but were generally not understood by those of European heritage. Therefore, Europeans often mistakenly considered prescriptions and treatments somewhat random. Still, most North American and South American physicians were equally well trained, systematic, and consistent in their protocols and patient diagnoses or prescriptions.

Consideration of the mind-body connection accepted and adopted by Western science and medicine only in the last half of the twentieth century was well established in the Americas centuries before they met Europeans. Because both pathogens and emotions can cause illness, Native Indians practiced holistic medicine to address not only the physical needs but social, psychological, economic, and spiritual, as well. Psychosomatic illnesses can have real physical symptoms induced by dreams, repressed thoughts, or mental processes, and Indigenous diagnoses may have recognized and considered those implications. Huron and Iroquois actively practiced what would centuries later be called dream-work psychology by Freudian and Jungian therapists and psychoanalysts.

Across the Atlantic from Europe was a brave new world which we are often only catching up with now, in our own version of this brave new world.

Teeth

Indigenous dentistry was developing between 1000 BC and AD 1000. They employed alum tooth whiteners, dental inlays, teeth-naming systems, dental hygiene, metal-tool tartar removal, and gum lesions prevention. They treated halitosis and tooth decay. They filled cavities and extracted teeth.

In dentistry, Aztec practices surpassed their 1492 European contemporaries. Mayan dental inlays in body remains are still intact in the patients' teeth after 2,000 years. Additionally, their complete dental implants from 1,300 years ago served as permanent, usable teeth, putting them on a par with today's technology. Even their saline solution rinse after a procedure resembles today's visits. The dentists placed an emphasis on oral hygiene with various toothbrushes, toothpaste, and mouthwashes.

Looking Around

When you look at your own day today, what is it you love about our way of life? The gifts of the American Indian are all around you. Remember, those contributions helped to form the foundations of today's civilization. The repeating pattern tells us we stood on the shoulders of the Indigenous in specialty after specialty after specialty, and then systematically erased the traces, eventually winding up where we are today, ignorant of the truth. A world-class education certainly doesn't seem to help when it comes to these areas of study. Lies are still abundant.

Unfortunately, the frightening news doesn't end there. There is further unpleasantness when we examine the future, and what we might expect in terms of change. First, let's acknowledge some progress.

Yes, there **has** been a lot of fantastic shifting in attitudes toward our continent's true inhabitants, except many of those changes come from wanting to jump the queue of Truth & Reconciliation. That is, let's skip over Truth and go straight to Reconciliation. Today, depending on which country of the Americas one lives in, the news can be saturated with the subject of Indigenous peoples. Heartrending news stories may cover the never-ending waves of fresh injustices, or they may be framed in a positive light as the new colonial methods are updated through the medium of "reporting." Our heartstrings may be pulled on by learning the Truth, but the feeling side is unsustainable, especially when it moves past tears into literally feeling sick to your stomach.

Reconciliation is the gain. Truth is the pain. But what have we always been told? No pain, no gain, right? Meaning... No Truth, no Reconciliation. We all want to avoid the pain of the Truth and jump straight to Reconciliation, but it won't work. Only embracing the truth will work, starting with less nauseating facts and more inspirational facts, like the ones contained in this book. Start with some simple recognitions and celebrations of Truth.

The frightening news I refer to is closely associated with the author's desperate desire to spread these messages now. Today's

...wanting to jump the queue of Truth & Reconciliation. That is, let's skip over Truth and go straight to Reconciliation.

one-shot sound-bite world may be succeeding in crystallizing a lot of the WRONG information in some drastic final gasp or twist of colonialism. Think about the internet examples, where technology is so bent on giving us new conveniences it prepackages our thinking for us. A quick invention date here, a first development there, and a thought placed in the right spot for us. Where does our machinery move on to after that?

SECTION 3

WHOSE CONTINENTS?

The upcoming generation will finally grow up in a world where people understand these two continents were stolen. Baby boomers normally have no idea what the term "settlers" even means, but university-age citizens customarily know the term and use the term to describe all of us who "came later." At least there is some good news. We have 4th World activists to thank for the increase in awareness.

The question is, are we going to wait for two generations to begin the real permanent fixes, or will we find a way to speed it up? Some of colonialisms' associated problems have created desperate situations. You hear it in the news, but may be filtering it through the lens of someone playing catch up. You might have even wondered, "Why are some millennial graduates calling everybody settlers?" You've never been given an opportunity to put Indian issues into perspective.

Well, nowadays you may learn from less-conditioned people you know or from youth who have been exposed to the unfairness of what transpired on these continents. You're getting your chance.

≋ CHAPTER 7 ≋
Eurocentric Views Then and Now

Europeans and Indians have never been on the same wavelength. A subtle tug of war has taken place over the centuries and continues today. It seems as if European traditions call for a certain type of behaviour, which has been reproduced in all of the various colonies around the globe. To restate these unspoken Eurocentric ground rules, "It's important to remember all of this was thought up over in White man's land." Also, "We were the far more advanced civilization whereas the cultures we dominated were more primitive." There are lots of variations, but the theme is the same. It's a contest beginning the moment any "superiority" example or issue is introduced. As soon as someone suggests similar levels of advancement, the game starts. The turf must be protected. The assumptions must triumph as fact. Within the contest, truth must favour the European team. It's worth remembering both civilizations thought the other peoples were backward and inferior in intelligence, considering the other to be more like children.

Eurocentric disconnect: agriculture

Considering the example of husbandry, when the Europeans came they saw agriculture practiced in a way quite foreign to them. There is still a view today you can find in history books. The belief is the Europeans came over and taught the Indians about agriculture. If one is aware of the real history of agriculture, the statement is ridiculous. It would be funny if it wasn't so tragic.

In Europe, they did have domesticated animals and fencing to contain their animals. But also, most of the continent in general was squared off and fenced off because of the noble system. The conditions under which the serfs and peasants lived meant they didn't often own their land. They certainly were not allowed to go on the land not assigned to them so most districts had a tendency to be cordoned off in order to limit all types of invasion and trespassing on the territory.

We know the Indians in South America and right up into North America grew their food very differently from Europeans and without fences or boundaries. In fact, it was grown much different than we grow food today. Food was most often grown as the three sisters grew, together, as in the story describing how one plant assists the other. Dirt mounds were used; rows were not.

When it came to producing food, there was a disconnect in the two civilizations' thinking.

There were food production systems on South American farms, called "milpas," where they would grow 10, 12, or 14 different plants all in one area. They would keep it weeded, if necessary, but to a European it looked disorganized. However, this is the way the Indian farms were designed and can still be seen today in some areas. Europeans persevered with their rows consisting of one type of crop. When it came to producing food, there was a disconnect in the two civilizations' thinking.

Eurocentric disconnect: language

Language and alphabets is another area where it's easy to see there is no connection between the Eurocentric view and the tradition of oral histories. Many cultures around the world have used oral histories, including several North American societies.

A North American "wampum" looking like beaded art to a Westerner might take eight or ten hours to be completely "read" by a skilled person with the knowledge and oral tradition. Often, language groups that could not speak directly to each other communicated through wampum strings or belts. A trained specialist from each group could facilitate a discussion or interpret messages using wampum. This is reminiscent of the way Chinese culture developed. Although there are over 200 spoken "Chinese languages," one written language serves them all today as a common communication tool.

It's difficult when you grow up the way we have to relate to a system which does not have an alphabet. There were some Western Hemisphere languages that had alphabetical systems, some with hieroglyphs, and some with knotted string systems, but we see the model for language fitting the same paradigm as food planting. There was a built-in assumption of superiority vs. backwardness.

In general, European colonizers were known to have outlawed Natives speaking in their own language, as many conquerors down through history have done. They outlawed customs, outlawed religious practices, and outlawed anything which might strengthen the society they were there to conquer.

Many of the Native language systems were disrupted by the Europeans. For example, most of the Mayan and Aztec accordion-shaped "codices" have been destroyed. Hundreds of these books were written prior to 1500. At one point, after the Spaniards had pretty much extracted all the information they wanted from the Mayan society, they made laws about burning all these books; this happened in 1562. In a similar pattern, varying laws were introduced all up and down the Western Hemisphere to try and disrupt the local administrations.

Religion was the reason given for destroying the codices and for outlawing native languages, in general. Local cultural practices always interfered with the Europeans' goals of conversion to Christianity. But Europeans were also primarily implementing a plan to conquer the people. While disease certainly helped them accomplish the intended result and played a huge part, millions of people were being killed, as well. Europeans were taking over these societies and their areas, and they did this by using force, making laws, and disrupting local administrative capacity through language laws.

The Mohawk language is an interesting example of a fundamental mismatch. In our language, we have the three tenses; past, present and future. These English tenses are also divided up to a small degree, but it's basically three time frames. Therefore, if something's happening "in the future," the tense indicates it "will happen."

The verb forms of the Mohawk language number into the twenties with most of them relating to the future. In many Indian cultures, there exists a 200-year timespan foundation to their thinking. Seven generations ahead is a very common reference with Indigenous. Evidence of seven generational thinking appears in the "Words Before All Else" spoken before important discussions in Kanienkeha (Mohawk language).

Many similar verb forms are built into Indian languages, indicating they tend to think seven generations ahead in their daily lives. This provides us with a snapshot of the difference in their mentality. They have a different view.

It's difficult trying to look at the unfolding history through the eyes of someone who speaks in that language with its 20-plus verb forms. We are unable to picture it. There is simply a lack of correlation between the Eurocentric view and some of the views of native peoples.

We cling to our choice of words and convenient notion that the many Indigenous "lost" their languages. No languages were lost. It implies some degree of carelessness over the generations, in failing to continue their interest in their Native tongue. Having them stolen and stripped away is the more accurate terminology.

Eurocentric disconnect: day-to-day indignities

The wheel, touched upon earlier, is another good example of the Eurocentric disconnect. The smoothness of European roads did not relate primarily to the wheel. Their thoroughfares were smooth partly to allow for horses, with their hooves and legs vulnerable to damage on uneven surfaces. The paths of South America, in particular, were designed for llamas, alpacas, and humans, all preferring uneven stepped surfaces on hilly winding routes. The Indigenous travel routes caused difficulties from the start, and Europeans complained bitterly, never able to reconcile the missing wheel. The wheel and the axle were available to the Indigenous, but it never occurred to them to make it widespread and use it in their technology mix. They didn't have the beasts of burden to carry loads and pull ploughs, and they had systems in place for ploughing their fields and doing it by hand. To the Europeans, it was another reason to treat them as savages.

We touched on cleanliness earlier. The second law Queen Isabella ever enforced in the original Hispaniola colony in 1494 made it illegal for the Indians to bathe themselves. This was because it was "very bad for their health," and they were doing it far too often, on at least a daily basis. The European visitors were known to smell to such an extent the island's inhabitants would not eat around them.

Christopher Columbus (real name: Cristobal Colon or Cristoforo Columbo) himself became governor of Hispaniola and was so well known for his mismanagement and brutal techniques he was eventually stripped of the position. Preoccupied with reinforcing Spanish authority at every turn, he ordered babies to be bashed against trees and killed, because he felt this was the way to subdue the inattentive natives. The full Tainos culture group in the West Indies, consisting of some eight million people before Spanish rule, was on the verge of becoming a nation state in 1492. Ten years later, they numbered 60,000 and had been practically wiped out.

The Spanish themselves wrote about their own early enslavement systems on the islands. The Tainos were immediately made to serve the Europeans' basic needs. In addition, the males became part of elaborate arrangements of labour and gold-searching expeditions. The sexual exploitation of the females was even more elaborate, modelling the existing slave trade and favouring girls of nine years old, whose value was highest among the different female age groups.

The Chinese were aware of the Europeans' ongoing plans for conquest. Where India, Africa, South America, and North America failed in defense of their homelands, China succeeded. Their word for Europeans translated to "savages," and Europeans were not even allowed to set foot in China. Dozens of vessels might be lined up waiting to trade, but the business was conducted through specialized brokers, while the people were forced to remain on board.

Famed explorer Martin Frobisher is best known for his search for a Northwest Passage, along with gold. He required no maps because he would lure Inuit kayaks close to his vessel then pluck them from the water, kidnapping people and forcing them to navigate through the waters. Europeans were well aware of the guide expertise within the thousands of tribes, and they kidnapped native residents to the extent an industry was created. Kidnapped enslaved mapping experts could be bought in Europe before a trip to the Western Hemisphere was even undertaken.

When the Europeans came along with their many expeditions, those early so-called explorers and settlers were after a quick buck. That's what they were doing. They were adventurers. Columbus' crew of 1,200 were released prisoners. They were short-sighted people living for the moment. It could be argued the quick-buck kind of mentality has never really ended in the 500 years since Columbus landed. Where is the gold? Let that concept stand alongside the princesses our daughters are preoccupied with imitating. Perhaps the get-rich-quick syndrome and the "pink aisle" toy stores signify the suggestion made previously that we are historically a society full of wannabe kings and queens longing to enrich ourselves and lord it over others.

Perhaps if each one of us was less concerned with suitable written details of the past or instant gratification now and more concerned with our legacy seven generations in the future, we could be passing on a more stable society today.

The mutual viewing lenses of the two civilizations just don't operate well together. We are so far apart in our cultural conditioning one could easily despair and conclude a genuine meeting of the minds is beyond our reach.

Among today's cultures, Western civilization in particular seems to want to remain on our chosen path of this comewhat-may desperate scrambling for progress. What about these Indigenous, these very accomplished cultures who seemed to be flourishing and doing quite well in 1492 in the Western Hemisphere?

≋ CHAPTER 8 ≋
Why Not Transform Some Attitudes and Worldviews?

I've said it before but I want to say it again, "All Europeans and Indians were peers and co-equals, but then people forgot."

You are being asked to transform some of your own worldviews and attitudes, and then transform the worldviews and attitudes of others. Let's increase our understanding and help those around us. Society's mainstream faulty attitudes are hurting us. They're hurting you. They're hurting the next generation. Yes... our inaccurate worldviews are ready to harm a whole new generation. But this time, the harm is expected to be deeper and more widespread. There's a shameful legacy about to be revealed and psychologists are already advising school teachers what to say to their students.

To transform our worldviews and their corresponding attitudes, we need to see a worldview in action. One example I use is the east coast of North America in 1492. The typical view is wildly off and simply wrong in most cases.

First off, what is a worldview? It's a mental model of reality, a framework of ideas and attitudes, a particular philosophy of life or conception of the world, as well as a comprehensive concept of the world from a specific standpoint. A worldview consists of a lot of images in a person's mind. One could almost nail someone's worldview down by asking them how they picture certain things. When asked about the Native Indian, you could likely go anywhere in the world and receive similar answers because the image of the Indian has been universally destroyed everywhere around the world.

You would receive similar answers to this fictitious questionnaire if you were to go to London, Johannesburg, Beijing, Bangkok, Cairo, Toronto, Lisbon, Moscow, New York, or Rio de Janeiro. You could probably go to most Indian reservations or communities, anywhere in North America or South America and find similar answers on "what was really happening here in 1492?" This information is not really on anybody's radar anywhere. But it's easily accessible. It's not really hidden. The issue is it has become invisible in our modern civilization.

So let's say, in this example, you're picturing the East Coast of North America in 1492. How do you generally think of that time period? What do you see in your mind? You'd normally think if you were going along there in a ship you'd see a lot of woods and that's about it, but that's not the reality. What would you really see if you were on the East Coast in 1492 or if you travelled there by ship in the 1500s as many did? The answer is you would see towns, smoke, homes, villages, signs of people, and cornfields 12 miles, 15 miles, and 18 miles long. It wasn't densely populated but there were people living there. It would be fairly obvious there were people living there.

This one example is useful when considering worldviews. It can cause you to wonder and ponder how did a faulty message end up as part of *my* world? Where did the pristine wilderness version come from in my past experiences? When did I receive it?

Indian inferiority

In our day-to-day lives, we can see the results of "Europeans and Indians were peers and co-equals, but then people forgot."

In our society, most of us tend to think everything comprising our daily lives derived from Europe. Adults still think the same today and kids are still being taught to believe those ideals. A history based upon European origins is built into our way of looking at the world. It's an assumption deeply ingrained in our culture and our words.

I want to address part of academia's underlying 500-year-long thesis stating Europeans are superior to everyone else. Let's examine the portion relating to the Western Hemisphere.

We know on Earth there is one landmass composed of Europe, Africa, and Asia, and there is a second landmass comprising North and South America. Does it make sense these two areas would develop over 20,000 years and one would come out as a bunch of primitive savages and the other would come out with all the advancements?

If you ask a child about the pyramids, even if he or she has never been taught about them in school, they'll more than likely say there are three, and they will know they are in Egypt. They haven't learned about Egypt; they haven't learned any of this. This is information they have just absorbed through cultural conditioning. We may "read between the lines" when we communicate in our personal interactions. Kids may "read between the lines" while exposed to conversation, television, or stories.

While it's true Egypt has 120 pyramids and Europe has a few dozen, what many people do not realize is there are over 1,000 pyramids in Mesoamerica alone, some of them larger and higher than the Egyptian pyramids. But nobody talks about that; we don't teach about it in school. It goes unnoticed. Somehow it remains uninteresting to those who both disseminate our information and those who control the dissemination. But this information will become interesting. It's going to become interesting as our collective fear subsides.

Educational systems are scrambling right now to try and rewrite history books for as early as next year. You can be sure they will not put a lot of this information in those books. That's already assured and predictable. This is not a situation whereby it's difficult to find information and compile the information, but it's not something we're willing to spread yet. The will is missing. So children will continue to miss out on a lot of fascinating truths.

Taking credit

Europeans take a lot of credit for "inventions" which don't rightfully belong to them. For instance, reading, writing, and arithmetic were not invented by the Europeans. Those were all invented by very dark-skinned races thousands of miles to the south and introduced into Europe.

Perhaps you take ownership of many things because of the colour of your skin. You want to emphasize the cradle of civilization and all that comes with the glorification of Eurasia's landmass. There is absolutely nothing wrong with that, but take ownership of all of it. When people pick and choose, they set the groundwork for all of the injustices that might follow; being proud feels good, and being ashamed feels bad.

There is also a contradictory foundation to the basis of our thinking. On the one hand, "we thought all this up" and will readily take the credit. On the other, when it comes to feeling accountable for actions hundreds of years ago, most people are confused even by the suggestion of it somehow connecting to them. "What does it have to do with me?" is the thinking. It is classic colonizer denial leading to our invisibility issues.

What about this idea "we thought all this up over there?" It's wrong to start with and very hypocritical. Is this redundant message getting noticed, wherein all the different races and cultures of the world have contributed equally to our civilization? No one can just say, "This is our civilization." Now is the time for us to accept culpability. Embrace the realities about any cruelty so you can move ahead and deal with the entire range of feelings and reactions.

One element of worldview holding people back from embracing the truth is the part which ties in with their religious beliefs. People in our society prefer to disassociate themselves from all aspects of the link between religion and wrongdoing. It's painful. There is a natural inclination to sugar coat any information which reveals wrongdoing on the part of organized religion. There is a failure to acknowledge the connection between the church of old and the church of today. So let's try being blunt.

The church helped organize the genocide of this continent's Indigenous people, and the church helped put the genocide into action. The church made the Inter Caetera Bulls and rules surrounding the genocide. The church acted as a referee between all of the factions fighting to benefit from the genocide. They sent their missions into Indigenous towns as a first move. Conversion to Christianity was a driving force behind all of the conquering, the brutality, and the manipulation.

...all the different races and cultures of the world have contributed equally to our civilization...

It was the church's insistence to put laws in place against language usage, pastimes, spiritual practices, cultural activities or recreation, and anything supporting the Indigenous populations in continuing their pre-existing way of life. Along the way, the conquerors pilfered many dozens of beneficial and advanced superior components of these civilizations. We still deal with the misinformation today.

So people living today may be guilty or uncomfortable to begin with, but when the aspect of religion is brought into the truthful accounts, even the progressives run for cover. Just when it seems impossible for the whole situation to become more complex, convoluted, and complicated, it is exactly what happens when the monkey wrench of religion is added to the mix.

When our past ancestral lineage or our country of origin proves to be problematic in some way, distancing ourselves in our minds is fairly simple. But for the average person, when their religion is difficult to relate to they cannot so easily treat it as a distant remote entity from the past.

Religion brings God into the picture. It's the same God all along, isn't it? This could be the part we do not want to go near. So the invisibility of the issues goes on and on with this additional enhancement.

We are all working to make our worldviews more accurate. We all would like our attitudes and actions aligned with our inner values. We all prefer to feel equal to others, not inherently superior. We all want children to have the best possible information. We all want to rest easy with our morality and our consciences.

Most individuals in the world appear to be wonderful human beings. We group ourselves together and create the actions making up current events and history. But what is it that happens to us when we group ourselves together and cause bad history to continue to unfold? That is one of our mysteries.

≋ CHAPTER 9 ≋
The Truth Behind
The Indian Legacy

As humans, we're running on software when we tie a shoe or drive a car, and we're running on software when we think. We are pre-programmed and conditioned.

What this means is you must remember the information you are receiving does not want to step past your firewall. It's tough to defeat your firewall; paradigms are almost impossible to overcome in our mind. Our belief systems are so strong information is literally blocked from moving through to our reasoning centres.

I ask you to focus in on one piece of information you love. Find a resonant image that keeps re-entering your awareness, one that amazes you or makes you realize something special was going on in your homeland thousands of years ago. Please come away with this one element when you leave.

Indians put the White man on the map.
So let's talk about some truth. The following paragraph is classic Ray Fadden.

Certainly, Indians put the White man on the map. When European men came to North and South America they moved their families and started settlements. Their children were crying because they were hungry, and it was the Indians who gave them corn, meat, and fish for their little ones. Indians were always a welcoming and considerate people, along 30,000 km of coastline. They considered others and were considerate of others.

They considered the animals as well. Another example of the difference between the Indians and the European settlers is shown in how the settlers treated the native animal populations. In the area of today's Eastern United States, ever since the settlers arrived, they put laws into place protecting the deer population. This was not because of the huge amount of people who later arrived. The White man would kill animals just for kicks.

For further illustration, there is an occurrence in the late 1800s which baffles the imagination. In a 13-year period, the White man killed three-to-four million buffalo per year. They were killing them because during that period of time buffalo skins were very popular, and they were killing them for the skins alone; the carcasses were normally left untouched.

For the sake of accuracy, the animals were actually bison. If you can picture the buffalo, his shoulder stands about as high as a person, 2.5 metres or ranging from 5 feet to 6.5 feet. One buffalo is a large thousand-pound creature. Picture just 1,000 buffalo and the amount of space they would take up and imagine the size of the whole operation to kill them, harvest their skins, and move them overseas. Then it becomes almost unimaginable to picture this entire operation; killing over 40,000,000 bison.

Furthermore, the American government sanctioned these slaughters because they were initiating a policy to move Plains Indians. The settlers felt little spiritual connection to the earth and to those animals, whereas the Native Indians had a deep-seated connection. The colonists' administration knew this and exploited that knowledge using the killing of the bison to try and weaken the Indigenous resolve.

All Indians' deep connection to earth and nature appears again and again, woven into the telling of historical events. The deep understanding of nature also led to many Western Hemisphere nations having more accurate calendars than their visitors. All of Europe was using the less-accurate Jovian calendar at the time.

All over the world, humans were sorting out time, the movement of heavenly bodies, and numbers themselves. The Mayans were first to use the zero as a number, well before it was independently discovered in the Mideast, and it was a monumental achievement in both cases. Along with the zero, Mayans had the disciplines of mathematics we have today: calculus, trigonometry, geometry, and algebra.

The Native Indians had and used several advancements before other parts of the world, which is not the point to sort of make it into a contest. The contest was not created by the Indigenous of the Western Hemisphere, by any means, and it was not created by me. But there are over 100 examples whereby they were actually more advanced than other areas of the world.

Then it becomes almost unimaginable to picture this entire operation; killing over 40,000,000 bison.

It's a European and Eurocentric thing to want to compare and make an overall contest regarding who was superior. It is the dominant culture that's done that, and now I'm certain they will eventually lose at their own game, because the Western Hemisphere was clearly more advanced. I no longer wait patiently for the day the contestants swap positions; I am taking action to make the changes I want to see. I say, "Let the contest begin." (In the back of my mind I recognize the urge for this contest may be a Euro-type urge in itself, coming from the White guy and colonizer mentality who still wants to test who's better.) We can agree it is not an issue to sort out who acquired something first. The issue has been created by the overall way our civilization exists.

Awkward teachings

Little children are not being given information concerning what really happened over the last 500 years. The truthful stories of the history are not proud. It's a shameful heritage, and when this information becomes more widely known it will be a difficult time for educators. But the process has begun. Some educational institutions are already taking the first steps to delicately expose the children to "new" truths.

Europeans, colonial governments, and colonial religions all left legacies that make people uncomfortable. Colonial religions were all guilty of making Indians ashamed of their people, their culture, and their traditions. When you make someone ashamed of their own grandfather and grandmother, you've done the worst harm to a person in the worst imaginable way. The person is lost and possibly lost forever. Try to imagine doing that generation after generation after generation for so long.

From the 1880s until the 1990s, generations of Indigenous peoples were forced to leave home to attend abusive religious Residential Schools, leading to the Truth and Reconciliation Commission and its long history in Canada. US Americans and

South Americans also imposed similarly harsh assimilation techniques. Today's schools organize Residential School field trips to raise awareness about the brutality of our ongoing colonial system. The visits to these fearsome buildings are becoming popular. Because the cruelty and mistreatment of these small Indigenous children is so recent, it can often leave the visiting children not only enlightened, but scared and confused.

It's difficult to explain in simple terms how this mistreatment could have happened. Indigenous Elders might remind us calmly of lives spent in effect imprisoned on reserves where a pass was required to receive permission to cross the "border" to the outside. The "60s scoop" and "baby-scoop era" are terms pointing to the kidnapping of 20,000 Indigenous Canadian children from the 1950s to the 1980s. The children, often taken at birth, were put up for adoption in Canada, United States and Europe, or placed in foster homes.

When school teachers cover these subjects, they are advised to take some time at the end of the class to address the psychological needs of the children. More grim truths will start to come out and be taught to kids more and more over the next 20 to 30 years. What reactions are we to expect from that generation of children when they are hammered with this shameful

...the kidnapping of 20,000 Indigenous Canadian children from the 1950s to the 1980s.

heritage? That's the reason it's not in the history books in the first place. These are not proud stories.

A great and long tragic story is of the Tuscarora Indian nation. What happened to them also happened to every Indian nation, eventually at the hands of White men.

The distasteful sagas begin with the original 1492 focus on Christopher Columbus. He set the stage. Statues of Columbus pop up all over the place, but why? He was a slave trader. He was a mass murderer. We have statues all over honouring him, particularly in the United States. In his documents, you can read what he said about the Indians on the very first page of his writing. He was amazed at the hospitality of the Indians and their attitude toward giving. "What they have they do not hesitate to share… an almost unbelievable generosity." But in the next few pages, you can see what type of a person he was, and the conquest and genocide he was planning for these people. So why do we celebrate a mass murderer?

Our children are going to be facing many hard truths in their lives and now they're going to have to deal with these historical truths. You have to feel sorry for your kids or grandkids. But even so, it's just information. I think we are a lot better off knowing.

Colonizer impunity

The time is coming to rewrite the history books.

Veracity will eventually show the colonial experience was unjust. History will embrace the unfortunate details of a forever interrupted Western Hemisphere. Societies will someday wonder why we lied about so many things. World citizens will admonish the Vatican for refusing at this late stage to denounce its earth-shattering 1452 and 1493 rulings.

An Inter Caetera Bull is a ruling passed down from the Pope, transferring his divine power to monarchies in every corner of Europe. Popes Nicolas V and Alexander VI, in their Inter Caetera Bulls, produced the edicts setting the stage for 550 years of Western domination. The documents gave permission in this ruling as follows: as long as they were there to convert the pagans, it was OK to kill natives, and take over their societies and belongings, and subjugate or enslave them. All the kings and queens then fell in line and followed the litany of colonize, convert, and enslave.

This official Doctrine of Discovery was and is part of the legal framework allowing European descendants to rule these lands. Today, we're still dealing with this Manifest Destiny, as it was also called in North America. Manifest Destiny says the long takeover was intended to happen. Caucasians were destined to triumph. It was certainly justified early on by Pope Alexander VI.

The attitude reached its peak during periods when disputes were settled with a uniquely colonial solution: we've just passed a law which says we can break Indian treaties whenever we want. That definitely settled all pesky negotiation issues.

For Canadians, you'd be interested to know how we are connected to South Africa, which becomes vilified for setting up apartheid in their country. When the South Africans were planning the setup of apartheid, they wanted to do research. At the time, the powers in charge, meaning the white powers, wanted to know how they could set this up and how they could go about doing it, and guess where they went to do research. They went to Canada, where the Indian Act has served a similar purpose from Confederation until today, failing to recognize the Indians as "persons."

We mentioned Blacks were not immune to all diseases, but they had already been exposed to malaria, so they didn't catch it. Twelve to 14 million Africans came to the Americas between 1500 and 1800. Incidentally, for every one slave stepping off the ship, five others perished during the entire horribly brutal process. Remember, this is another invisible part of history when you think of those 60 to 70 million dead Africans.

There were only a few White people, three to four million Europeans, but 12 to 14 million Black people came during that time. Therefore, the average person in the Americas was either Black or Indigenous. Much of the real narrative of the Americas involves the interaction of these two peoples.

Between two and four million Indians were also sold and forced into slavery. Regarding the Indians sold into slavery, what happened typically in North America was a Black slave would be purchased while the Indian slaves were sold down in the West Indies. By bringing in a Black slave, they likely avoided a situation of having Indian slaves working for them with that slave's village potentially being in a neighbouring land. This is another set of information lost and forgotten.

CHAPTER 10

What You Can Do

Reach into your wallet

Honing in on more Canada-specific examples, we can look at the scandals making the daily news. The National Inquiry into Missing and Murdered Indigenous Women and Girls is recent news, but the problem has existed throughout colonial history. The "60s" scoop was 40 years before. The Residential Schools takes us back 40 years before then.

Looking back at history you start to realize every 40 years we've been doing something just as bad. New scandals are waiting to be uncovered and highlighted. The problems of discrimination and tyranny are not just recent. These problems have existed for the last 400 or 500 years, and the issues are not going away.

And by the way, it was wrong. Take the bags off your heads and see that it was wrong.

Repairing our society is going to cost money. If every one of about 22 million Canadian taxpayers holds up four 100-dollar bills, the total amount would not quite cover the "60s" scoop lawsuit; one small lawsuit. This sample amount makes only a small dent in the entire compensation picture within Canada.

Additionally, the compensation picture I refer to represents only one country out of 35 within these two continents. Furthermore, even that discussion comprising only costs for direct damages from wrongdoing is also a small dent in a larger question... what is the entire combined theft amount from the land itself, along with oil, gas, minerals, wood, and all other resources extracted from those Indian lands? To be clear, the upcoming answer is not intended to be in any way hyperbolic or melodramatic.

Quadrillions and quadrillions.

Look to this answer if you wonder why governments are timid when it comes to being completely truthful.

More importantly, this is also going to cost psychological health. We stole everything, folks. There are repercussions when you steal. Don't we all know this? It can be pretty nice for a while. But then the school principals come to give everybody the strap, don't they? Those who steal never get away scot free.

People do not seem to comprehend the situation we are facing today. We have tens of thousands working hard to correct the issues we created for the Indigenous, and I thank every single one. We have Truth and Reconciliation Commissions. We have the United Nations Declaration on the Rights of Indigenous Peoples. But do we perceive what's really happening? Examined through my 1492 lens, our entire way of life is founded on lies and transgressions.

North American Indians overall are left today with around 2% of their lands and struggle to hang onto that. In Canada, the ownership is more extreme: 99.8% compared to 0.2%; 1/5 of 1%.

Where does one even start? We as a civilization are slowly going back 40 years at a time to reveal these painstaking discoveries and gradually admit complicity. But why do we keep unveiling each 40-year injustice and pretending the big picture can be dealt with entirely and conclusively? We deceive ourselves by thinking, "Finally, resolving ALL of these injustice issues is just around the corner."

Euro-speak can be heard imbedded in our news broadcasts and feature stories. You hear things such as "...this dark period in our history is finally being dealt with..." We use these words to convey our hopes this anomaly will finally be confronted, it will all be over quickly, there will be a big sigh of relief, and we can all move forward. But the truth of the entire history is hidden in the dark!

What does Truth and Reconciliation start with? It's very simple; it starts with Truth.

Let's go BACK TO THE BEGINNING and face the foundational truths. My point is there is so much noise on the subject of Indigenous peoples, but still no one seems to realize what is happening.

The Native Indians were more advanced than the visiting Europeans. Yet we perpetuate a false history. We conquered them. We stole their land. We hijacked their information. We burned all their books. We disrupted their administrative systems. We passed laws forbidding them to use their languages or culture. We rewrote the history books with falsehoods.

There are repercussions when you steal. Don't we all know this?

Captain Kirk was always able to come to an area with a far more advanced civilization and somehow prevail, wasn't he? That's the classic tale. He and his newcomers, by using wiles and guile and Western ways would eventually find a way to overtake the folks they were visiting. Kirk saw this as simple and natural and self-evident, and we explain our own conquests in these simple terms, too. We have even embellished the stories over time.

Now both the stories and the embellishments are being scrutinized. Coming to grips with present day is not as easy as reaching into our wallets and quickly paying to solve a range of issues. We are compelled by our collective ethics and our sense of decency to reach further and travel further.

First Nations in Canada

I want you to consider some details on an uncomfortable subject, something difficult to wrap your head around. By creating the term First Nations in Canada, the power structure inadvertently removed our Canadian Indigenous from their race and the history and heritage of those Peoples. It attempts to make them Canadians first and foremost. Instead of identifying themselves with everything going on in 1492, they became shut off behind a European imaginary line (Canada) and failed to share in being proud of what all Indians accomplished. On the other hand, the White man takes credit culturally and racially for every contribution of Caucasians, regardless of what era or location.

Exciting and inspiring Indigenous groups are at last collectively forming in North America, joining Central American, South American, and world Indigenous movements. It's an activist network just now entering mainstream consciousness. While they struggle to connect on identical-looking problems, governments struggle to slow them down or stop them. Under the guise of awarding rights to Indians, dominant-culture governments still attempt to legislate Indians out of existence.

In other words, the punctilious First Nation designation with its political correctness might be one of the next things we are doing to "help" them, but it appears to fit the permanent pattern. It makes the White establishment feel better at the moment but it potentially cuts the Native people off from part of their true selves. In this case, the ancestors of hundreds of pre-colonial Peoples call themselves Indians. But in Canada it's being politicized out of existence. It's not just happening here. In Australia, a similar situation exists with the term Aboriginals.

Here's another more complex way to describe the creeping regression around the terminology First Nations, a description so central it is somewhat forbidden in Canada to use other terms in polite company. There is an assumption in history; ignorance and hate lead to racist ideas, and racist ideas lead to the racist economic policies, shutting out the non-mainstream members of society. Therefore, if we tackle racism at its people-focussed source we can combat the ignorance and hate. Dealing with these issues will lead to combating racist ideas, which will then lead to combating racist economic policies. In other words, if we fix the root problems of discrimination, economic opportunities will flow to those that were previously shut out. Makes good sense, right?

The problem is the model is backward and upside down and wrong. Unlock this issue and you then unlock some of the reasons for the slow pace of the struggle against colonial domination. OK, so why is it backwards?

The correct order should be racist economic policies which were put in place strictly for profits, led to racist ideas, and racist ideas led to ignorance and hate; **NOT** ignorance and hate led to racist ideas, and racist ideas led to racist economic policies. The difference is critical.

Only the actions changing the economic policies will have impact. All of the injustice stems from the business side; the visible racism is a byproduct of the racist economic systems. Changing racism is certainly important, but will never lead to equal opportunities or meaningful change.

We are speaking about Indigenous, but consider slavery for a moment. Africans weren't considered inferior, which led to racist ideas, which led to the racist economic policies of the worldwide slave trade. It worked in the opposite way. The economic policies were racist. The policies eventually led to racist ideas being introduced into the equation as a justification for the actions. The racist ideas over time led to hate and ignorance toward Black populations.

Hate and ignorance is still around today for Blacks, just as it is for the Indigenous. But the fight for change must be undertaken at the economic level, if results are to be achieved. Follow the money!

Europeans have coveted the land and resources through these hundreds of years, and they found ways to exploit the original owners and take those economic advantages for themselves. These racist economic policies led to the introduction of racist ideas, reflexively created along the way as a way to explain their actions. Then over time the racist ideas took hold, until ignorance and hate toward Indians became widespread.

Whites need help

Europeans have had a long history of settling their differences by blood and war. The centuries leading up to 1492 were no different with dozens of border changes and the killing which goes along with those campaigns. Europeans were a vicious war-like race of people who went across the ocean in search of gold.

I've already laid out many reasons why Europeans were not superior. That troupe is old news yet still the invention of steel is routinely trotted out as the main evidence for European superiority at least on all things technological. History ignores the fact the iron was scarce in the Western Hemisphere; it ignores the fact some Indigenous had iron tools to go with their other metal tools, but let's not ignore the driving force behind the European advancements – warfare.

Now 500 years have gone by, and we're still a vicious warlike people in search of gold. It's difficult to be convinced otherwise. Is it guns, germs, and steel making the difference? Or is it greed, audacity, and brutality?

No other creature routinely kills its own kind as humans do, but we have made a business out of it. Doing this takes it to a new level. Paying for Indian scalps takes the viciousness to a new level. If you still need more evidence of our warlike attitudes take a look around. Who could forget torpedoes, submarines, napalm, germ warfare, concentration camps, chemical warfare, atomic bombs, machine guns, bombers, or miniature targeted drone guns with facial recognition software? If it is for killing, we have thought of it.

The Whites need help right now. Forget about sending their missionaries all over the world for the last thousand years. They need to send someone among their own people. It's time to leave the Indians and other peoples alone. Whites need to be taught right from wrong and then remember to follow the teachings when the time comes. They're so smug and think they know everything because they begin to believe their own propaganda and lies in the history books. They love to hearken back to the cradle of civilization, the Fertile Crescent kids are expected to think of as the beginning of our way of life. There is an arrogance that sums up my White dilemma. The cradle of civilization is a myth of the master race, ladies and gentlemen. It's time to move forward.

This book is for Whites. They have the integrity problem, touched upon earlier, which is soon coming home to roost. The sooner they deal with it the better. Will you be teaching your kids we stole everything? They would have a head start, at least. Young generations are about to be hammered with this information. The stories are not proud, which is why they've become invisible. These generations are being left to clean up a lot of messes.

A leading factor in all this mess is the education system's handling of the Western Hemisphere because education system paradigms go to the root of who we are and what we believe. Messing up the earth can result in soul searching, but the scale of a systematic 500-year genocide carried out on one of our four races is difficult to pass off as inattention.

So this is a treatise for Whites? What about all the Native Indian emphasis? The gifts? The extraordinary contributions by Indians? The truths? The correcting of bad info about all things Indigenous? Surely this book is an effort on behalf of correctness. Surely this is an effort on behalf of Indians.

Correctness? Yes. Indians? No.

Here's why it can never be an effort on behalf of the true inhabitants of South, Meso-, and North America. When a White person or a Whitened person sets out to "help" Indians, it is assured from the outset they are either hindering Indians, helping their own cause, seeking an advantage, making themselves feel better, or reacting knee-jerk style. It's more likely to be all of the above.

The stories are not proud, which is why they've become invisible.

The hijacking of Indigenous traditions by opportunistic White colonizers has existed since the time of Columbus. Many recent examples in our culture resulted in similar outcomes of bogus representations and harm to the Indigenous – Carlos Castaneda, Brooke Medicine Eagle, Jamake Highwater, Ruth Beebe Hill, Lynn Andrews, David Seals, Mary Summer Rain, or Sam D. Gill. I encourage you to look up their stories. Each of these names represents a unique story, but all follow a common theme; the appropriation of all things native lurks in the background at all times.

Can we please just stop "helping" them for a generation or two while we acquire some basic information? With the next education campaign, let us target the correct people this time; Whites, not Indians! A look inward wouldn't hurt, while we're at it. Then when that's done, maybe an additional ignorance check.

When you hear the word "helping" you can be certain it means "our solution." It's a solution to benefit the mainstream White population. Learn some historical truth, listen to our 4th World hosts, and start paying attention to the things *they* ask for; don't reach beyond toward "helping."

Help yourself instead. We need it.

It goes like this. YOU [original inhabitant of these continents] have a complaint, and you have expressed it. WE [visitor, guest, intruder, other] have a diagnosis. Here's the remedy. We will hit you on the head with this mallet. When you have recovered from the treatment in 40 years, we will be ready to help you again. We're going to keep helping you every 40 years until things are fixed when you no longer need to come forward with a complaint and express it. It's then when we can be triumphant in our altruism knowing the treatment was a success.

I'll be no doubt wielding the mallet, right here in the writing of this book, without even wanting to or trying. It's inescapable at this late date. To put it another way, it's already probable this

With the next education campaign, let us target the correct people this time; Whites, not Indians!

effort will be framed as "helping Indians." It will accidentally be seen as "helping" without my approval or involvement. Rest assured I would not formulate a plan to do it on purpose. Why would I set out to intentionally swing the mallet?

OK, so that's clear? Nothing's on behalf of Indians. It's an oxymoron, with the hypocrisy built in. Move forward in your worldview with some truth from these pages, knowing full well there is an avowed and admitted pretense this message is for Whites. It's for everybody; all races and sub-races and cultures and subcultures, pay attention. Speaking of Non-Whites, the premise "we thought all this up over there in Europe" still excludes other races and cultures.

So how does this book apply to all of the Non-Caucasians who make up such a chunk of our populations in the twenty-first century? There's a sort of exemption for them within my main message "all Europeans and Indians were peers and co-equals in 1492 but then people forgot." Cultures of all stripes can fall back on the same old standard, "OK, interesting, but it's got nothing to do with me."

Anyone who has come to North America can still take credit for starting our civilization. They do it with their worldview by extending the European practice to the LAND MASS itself.

The message becomes "everything good and great had to come from the OTHER LAND MASS," instead of just Europe. Whether they come from Asia, the Mideast, the Orient or elsewhere, the message still stands. This brings in the pyramids and writing and the cradle of civilization and a whole range of myths to continue perpetuating Indians-as-primitives thinking.

Thus, we see the central problem extending beyond just the White immigrants; lots of diverse immigrants are in on the act without missing a beat. This is an important point which had bothered me for awhile but now I have it worked out. Everything in this book can apply to them while they are employing these usual habits.

And by the way, Blacks are NOT included in "we thought all this up over there," because the shameful legacy makes them invisible, too. It's ironic *they* are not included, since North Africa and the Mideast are known to have had many influential ancient Black cultures. A lot of progress for humans came from those areas. Today, other Non-Blacks join with Whites in the age-old assumptions Blacks couldn't have been instrumental in ancient accomplishments and history. Blacks get short-changed with many people actually believing Egypt isn't really even part of Africa. The contributions I'm referring to, often Black gifts to the world, actually allow immigrants from the OTHER LAND MASS to take credit in their minds, maintain these habits of thinking, and continue the spread of faulty worldviews. That's the irony referred to.

This book is not the work of a footnoting academic. More accurately, it's the scribblings of an angry pop historian who is tired of doing rants in his car. In this era of conspiracy theories, might I submit we have a whopper right in front of us?

The Europeans were searching for gold, remember? The running of the papal bulls was in full gallop. The way was officially cleared for the sanctioned subjugation of native populations in the new areas. As long as the aim was called "conversion to Christianity," killing the heathens was OK, stealing from the heathens was OK, and subduing the heathens was OK.

Once the pope gave the green light in his Papal Bull of 1493, squeamish kings and queens everywhere could sleep easy. The mayhem was part of a grander plan. God was involved. After all, divine rights counted for something.

What bothers me? People let themselves get hit with guilt every day in the news when they could be free. Let's deconstruct the lies, create the truth, and lead the life of understanding. Please help. Help people understand the facts, understand their outer world, understand their worldview, understand their own situation, understand their inner self, and then understand their soul.

Help yourself. It's time to uncover the 500 years of lies and understand the truth of the American Indian. Only then can you experience your own personal truth and reconciliation.

≋ CHAPTER 11 ≋

Wrap-Up

When we look at our own core values as individuals, each one of us must decide which ones come first and which ones are not on our list. Core values are placed in an order of importance. Your values are your simplest decision-making tool. When day-to-day decisions are made we look at our core values and behave accordingly.

Do your values include wealth accumulation, protection of your own belief system, guarding society against people, or declining the choice to embrace differences?

Will it be honesty, integrity, tolerance, fairness?

For those of you who deem **fairness** as an important core value, the information in this book will resonate with you. It's not fair we all live with lies when the truth is available. It's not fair we all grow up with worldviews which teach us very little of importance was accomplished in the Western Hemisphere until Europeans came.

If it's not fair, there isn't a way to sugar coat it so it looks fair. I often hear from people who ask if I'm Indigenous because they wonder or want to know why I would care so much about these issues if I'm not Indigenous. Where I see hundreds of Native contributions colouring my view of the world, there are countless many in our populations who see only one or two gifts (usually corn). The same "one-contribution worldview" dominates much of our societal collective worldview.

Does it matter? Is the issue human beings in thousands of Indigenous cultures around the world have been mistreated? Is the issue we don't know how to resolve colonial complications? Could the issue be the one-contribution worldview asks, "What do they want, anyway? What are the Indigenous after? Can't they move?"

OK, so some folks just don't understand. They choose not to understand it. Their ancestors came here. What does all this have to do with them? There's nothing wrong with their thinking, but there's nothing right about it, either. When it's pointed out to you, "Hey, you are taking credit for your ancestors' cool stuff, but won't take credit for the bad stuff," are you stretching your mental ligaments to try to *understand* it, or are you compiling excuses for yourself?

Would you at least listen to someone who answers the question, "Why would you care about these subjects?" It's because of fairness. The status quo is NOT FAIR currently, but it's not difficult for you to make it fair. The people I meet who kick and scream about their adjusted worldviews can fight against their body's own physiology which does not want contrary thoughts entering. We're designed that way. Our biology and our brain activities are trying to protect us against new and scary input, every minute of every day.

But you can override the blocking of new information. If fairness is one of your core values, you will be successful.

As a minimum, you can at least spread the message within yourself.

Let's be FAIR.

≋⊩ Afterword ⊪≋

Are my readers sometimes disappointed when they look for my annotations? Sure. Those readers are justified when they characterize my work, in their minds, as history. For you, I recommend shifting your mental bookstore way down toward the self-development section. It's where this book fits in; yes, one more self-help book.

The purpose of "500 Years of Lies: Discover the Extraordinary Number of Native Indian Gifts to the World" is to provide a quick slap to wake up sleeping worldviews. I have no difficulty with being accused of running off at the mouth while stubbornly providing no proof. I say, "Fine, at least you were engaged if you found yourself up-in-arms defending your traditional worldview."

So many thousands of lies have been told about Native Indians, even a book trying to exaggerate and make unsubstantiated claims could never match the totals. Fortunately, there is a vast amount of accurate knowledge available today, but it hasn't been produced by mainstream academics.

What have *they*, the mainstream historians, educators, and scientists been doing? To give some credit, perhaps they have been making adjustments to their blinders over these 20 generations. Like all of us in this dominant-culture world, they do their best. They really think they're trying, but even if they are adjusting, they bother me.

Historians have provided the official network of lies that backup the unfair treatment of these 3,500 peoples of the world. Educators have instilled the supremacist values in each new wave of youngsters. Anthropologists have distorted their findings to assure emerging facts support existing frameworks of thought. Archaeologists don't bother me nearly as much, but they do step into plenty of troubles over their disrespectfulness. Maybe they don't understand it, but it doesn't mean they make things worse on the faulty-worldview front. Archaeologists have actually improved the situation by providing new tidings.

Those who reinforce the entrenchment of the dominant worldview need to change. Let's target the official perpetrators of the myths, target the enablers, the politicians, the academics, and the policymakers who rubberstamp the perpetrators. They are *entrenchers*. Even you and I are not free from blame.

In my own example, being a White, middle-class kid from southern Ontario, I'm part of the problem. I was *entrenched* in these beliefs, which normally involves working to *entrench* others. That is what an *entrencher* is. I am a colonizer, designed from birth to entrench silly ideas about Indians. I accept it. Join me and spread the message to four people. Try owning it. Admit to your complicity, and then begin searching for the *entrenching* contained within your own parenting. Stretch yourself and begin recognizing it.

Will some annotations help the whole effort? Possibly, and maybe someday an expanded version will sport them. For now, I'll be blunt in my self-assessment.

At my speaking events, I always find a place to prominently display two books:

Encyclopedia of American Indian Contributions to the World – 15,000 Years of Inventions and Innovations – by Emory Dean Keoke and Kay Marie Porterfield

1491: New Revelations of the Americas before Columbus
– by Charles C. Mann

Although I am definitely not an academic, I absolutely love reading and digging and researching my narrow subject. The enclosed book list highlights only my favourites.

When it comes to giving my live presentations, I'm sure 80% of my work could be performed by having **just** those two books. Do you see? The information isn't the difficulty. The issue is not the facts being in dispute. That is a red herring, utilized by the kicking and screaming two-thirds of the population that will not *yet* accept my message. The invisibility is the issue. I am hoping the 80% figure reinforces this point. Actually, I have usually given the figure as 90% when I'm chatting with audience members after an event.

Listen: The fascinating truth is only a few clicks away for all of us pop historians.

—**Dave Patterson**, *the1492guy*

⧉ Suggested ⧈
Reading

To maximize the usefulness of this book list, these selected works appear in order of priority, rather than in alphabetical order. Therefore, the ones nearer the top represent my opinion of the most impactful picks for readers wanting to dive into the subjects covered in "500 Years of Lies."

Mann, Charles. *1491: New Revelations of the Americas before Columbus.* Vintage Books. New York, NY. 2005.

Keoke, Emory Dean and Kay Marie Porterfield. *Encyclopedia of American Indian Contributions to the World – 15,000 Years of Inventions and Innovations.* Facts on File. New York, NY. 2002

Weatherford, Jack. *Indian Givers: How the Indians of the Americas Transformed the World.* Crown Publishers. New York, NY. 1988.

Manuel, Arthur & Grand Chief Ronald M. Derrickson. *Unsettling Canada: A National Wake-up Call.* Between the Lines. Toronto, ON. 2015.

Morgan, Lewis Henry. *League of the Ho-de-no-sau-nee or Iroquois.* Corinth Books, 1862 reprint. New York, NY. 1851.

Wallace, Paul A. W. *The White Roots of Peace.* Clear Light Publications, 1994 reprint. Santa Fe, NM. 1946

Dunbar-Ortiz, Roxanne & Dina Gilio-Whitaker. *"All the Real Indians Died Off" and 20 Other Myths about Native Americans.* Beacon Press. Boston, MA. 2016.

Manuel, Arthur & Grand Chief Ronald M. Derrickson. *The Reconciliation Manifesto: Recovering the Land, Rebuilding the Economy.* James Lorimer & Company, Ltd. Toronto, ON. 2017.

Dunbar-Ortiz, Roxanne. *An Indigenous Peoples' History of the United States.* Beacon Press. Boston, MA. 2014.

Weatherford, Jack. *Native Roots: How the Indians Enriched America.* The Random House Publishing Group. New York, NY. 1991.

Waziyatawin (formerly Wilson, Angela Cavender). *For Indigenous Eyes Only: A Decolonization Handbook.* School for Advanced Research Press. 2005.

Vega, Garsilaso de la. *The Incas.* Avon. New York, NY. 1961.

Wright, Ronald. *Stolen Continents.* Houghton Mifflin. New York, NY. 1992

Akwesasne Notes, ed. *Basic Call to Consciousness.* Reprinted by Book Publishing Co. Rooseveltown, NY. 1986

Grinde, Jr., Donald A. & Bruce E. Johansen. *Exemplar of Liberty: Native America and the Evolution of Democracy.* University of Los Angeles, American Indian Studies Center. Los Angeles, CA. 1991.

Colden, Cadwallader. *The History of the Five Indian Nations of Canada, which are Dependent on the Province of New York in America.* T. Osborne. London, England, 1747.

Stannard, David E. *American Holocaust: Columbus and The Conquest of the New World.* Oxford: Oxford University Press. New York, NY. 1992.

Mann, Charles C. 1493: *Uncovering the New World Columbus Created.* Vintage Books. New York, NY. 2011.

Brown, Dee. *Bury My Heart at Wounded Knee: An Indian History of the American West.* Henry Holt & Company, LLC. New York. 1970.

<+o————————————————————————o+>

About the1492guy

Professional speaker Dave Patterson "the1492guy" reaches audiences across North America with his mix of passion, fun, practical communication, positivity, and understanding. When you attend the1492guy's presentation, get ready to go back in time and gain a new perspective. The experience will have you looking at the amazing narratives from an exciting new point of view, filling in critical knowledge gaps. Without going back to a point of origin and correcting many misconceptions, the problem-solving and complaints processes of today may be doomed to keep repeating the same errors and flawed solutions.

Dave's 5 Steps To
Your Own Personal Truth & Reconciliation

1. Realize that Europeans and Indians were peers and co-equals — but then people forgot
2. Learn so you can share your surprise
3. Love our way of life
4. Transform worldviews
5. Become guilt-free

<+o————————————————————————o+>

Stay in touch and share the message

You can find Dave's speaking schedule and list of appearances on the site. As always, he's thrilled if you can go share your experiences or new narratives with a minimum of four people, and send them to Dave's site so they can stay in touch. If they argue with you, send them directly to Dave so he can straighten them out!

TO BOOK DAVE FOR SPEAKING
Call 800.250.7955 or email
bookings@the1492guy.com

Visit the website and sign up for Dave's mailing list. Get regular updates, videos, and other news.

www.the1492guy.com

@the1492guy   the1492guy   the1492guy   the1492guy

Subscribe to Dave's YouTube channel at the1492guy.

CPSIA information can be obtained
at www.ICGtesting.com
Printed in the USA
LVOW13s2021100618
579585LV00003BA/3/P